KALI LINUX:

Table of Contents

Introduction

Hacking is like cooking. You need to get ready with all the ingredients (i.e. programs) and know in detail about the properties of that ingredients (or programs) and use them together to produce a culinary material. What if the food doesn't taste good? That is if you are unable to get the better results after all the hacking process? There is only one way you can do i.e.; to try again.

There are five important areas you need to learn in detail to master hacking.

1) Information Gathering

2) Automatic Vulnerability Scanning

3) Exploiting

4) Password Attacks

5) Sniffing and wireless attacks

1) Information gathering

Information gathering is always considered a pivotal job hacker should do before attacking a target. It roughly sums up that by using information gathering tools we can acquire a lot of information about the target hosts, which can help us create exploits that would help us create a backdoor for further exploitation. We can even use tons of publicly available information about the target to get a good idea on what strategy we should use to make this attack successful.

2) Automatic Vulnerability scanning

Vulnerability Scanner is a program that automatically finds and discovers security vulnerabilities in computers, network applications, web applications and software. It detects the target system through the network, generates data to the target system, and matches the feedback data with the built-in vulnerability signature database to enumerate the security vulnerabilities existing on the target system. Vulnerability scanning is an indispensable means to ensure system and network security. In the face of Internet intrusion, if users can detect security vulnerabilities through network scanning as soon as possible according to the specific application environment, and timely take appropriate measures to repair, it can effectively prevent the occurrence of intrusion events. Because the work is relatively boring, we can implement it with some convenient tools, such as Nessus and OpenVAS.

3) Exploiting

Exploiting is an important way to gain control of the system. The user finds a vulnerable vulnerability from the target system and then uses the vulnerability to obtain permissions to control the target system. In order to facilitate the user's practice, this chapter will introduce Metasploitable 2 released by Metasploit. Users can use it as a Linux operating system for practice. This chapter will use the vulnerabilities on the Metasploitable system to introduce various penetration attacks, such as MySQL database, PostgreSQL database and Tomcat service.

Privilege escalation is to maximize the minimum privilege a user has. Often, the users we gain access to may have the lowest permissions. However, if you want to perform a penetration attack, you may need the administrator account permissions, so you need to increase the permissions. Permission elevation can be achieved by using fake tokens, local privilege escalation, and social engineering.

4) Password Attacks

A password attack is to recover the password plaintext without knowing the key. Password attacks are an important part of all penetration testing. If you are a penetration tester and don't understand passwords and password cracking, it's hard to imagine. So, no matter what you do or how far our technical capabilities are, passwords still seem to be the most common way to protect data and restrict access to the system. This chapter describes various password attack methods, such as password online attacks, router password attacks, and creating password dictionaries.

5) Sniffing and wireless attacks

This is where people use wireless network tools along with a network adapter to capture packets and crack password or acquire sensitive information from the target. Sniffing tools like Wireshark are famous and can be used for a lot of attacks and finding out the packets.

Information Gathering

Information gathering is an important pre attack phase where the hackers collect a lot of information that is available in public about the target he is going to attack. Many hackers use social engineering techniques to get a solid bunch of information about target and the technology it is using along with the operating system and version it uses. Every hacker uses different set of methodologies to create a good information about the host before targeting.

There are three important phases in information gathering as explained below

1) Gathering information from search engines

Use search engines like Google to get good information about the host you are trying to attack. You will be surprised with the fact that how much you can find information that is public.

2) Social engineering techniques

Social engineering techniques are crazy because you can just psychologically trick an employee or the target you are chasing with a simple thing like phishing email to create a backdoor via your exploit. All great hackers rely on social engineering instead of doing things in a more complex way.

3) Port Scanning

If you are curious to know about what a port scan is associated with follow the next few paragraphs carefully. There are various services provided by the server, such as publishing a home page and sending and receiving e-mails.

Services that perform network communication include a window called "port" for communication, which is managed by numbers. For example, well-known services are basically pre-assigned port numbers, such as 80 for HTTP services that publish their home pages on the Internet and 587 for sending emails.

The act of investigating from the outside (attacker point of view) that what kind of port the server is opening is called "port scan".

How a port scan be done?

Port scanning is the process of sending specific data from the outside and examining the corresponding responses in order to investigate the running services on servers connected to the network. By analyzing the response obtained, you can identify the version of the service running on the server, the OS, etc.

Nmap

Nmap is one of the famous hacking tools and is widely known for its popularity among penetration testers. People often mistake that Nmap is only popular for its information gathering abilities but often doesn't understand that Nmap can also be used as a vulnerability detector that can be automated. It can be used in various operating systems that are open source and in Windows.

Nmap is a powerful tool that can be used for port discovery, host discovery, service discovery, detection of operating system and its version. Nmap can be used in both command line and with graphical user interface (GUI). But remember that good hackers use the Command line.

How Nmap works?

Nmap is programmed in a way such that it can perform scanning using different technologies like TCP and FTP protocol scans. All these scans are prone to their strengths and weaknesses and hackers can understand it vividly when they are trying to attack hosts with Nmap.

In hacking terminology, we call the target technically as the target host. When using Nmap we need to first understand the complexity of target to decide which scan to use either simple easy scan or a complex scan that would take a lot more time. We need to polish our skills to use some very complex and intuitive techniques to get past from intrusion detection systems to get good results.

Below are some strategies that will help you appreciate various operations Nmap can perform:

1) You can scan a single host with the following command

nmap www.hackingtools.com

nmap 192.232.2.1

2) You can scan an entire subnet with the following command

nmap 192.232.2.1/24

3) Nmap can also be used to scan multiple targets with the following command

#nmap 192.232.2.1 192.232.2.4

4) There is also an option in Nmap that will let you scan a range of targets as follows

#nmap 192.232.2.1-100 (This in precise scans every host that is in between the IP addresses 192.232.2.1 and 192.232.2.100)

5) Nmap has an option where you can store all the Ip addresses you have in a text file that is in .txt format and place in the same directory of Nmap so that it can

scan every IP address present in the text file without manually entering each one of them.

#nmap -iL sampleip.txt

6) If you want to see a list of all the hosts you need to scan you can enter the following command

#nmap -sL 192.232.2.1/24

7) Nmap provides an option where we can exclude a single IP address from scanning with subnet hosts

#nmap 192.232.2.1/24 -exclude 192.232.2.4

And if you want to exclude more than one IP, you can include all of them in a text file so that they can be excluded while doing the subnet scan like shown below.

#nmap 192.232.2.1/24 -exclude excludeIp.txt

Before learning about the scanning procedures Nmap offers let us know about scanning ports on a specific host. You can scan individual ports in a host using the following command.

#nmap -p78,56,23 192.232.2.1

Scanning technology in Nmap

There are different types of scanning strategies that Nmap follows to do the work. In this section, we will describe about these procedures in detail along with few commands that will give you a good overview.

1) sS scan (Tcp SYN)

This is a typical scan that Nmap uses if nothing is specified by the hacker to the software. In this scan usually, Nmap will not give a full handshake to the target system. It will just send an SYN packet to the target host, which will then check for any open ports, but not creating any sessions that may be used after logging. This is one of the greatest strengths of this scanning strategy. To use this scan the hacking tool should be given root access otherwise it will show an error. Below we give the command line for this scan.

hacking@kali #nmap -sS 262.232.2.1

2) sT scan (TCP connect)

If the sS scan is not used due to the reason that it is not feasible for the current attack situation people normally use sT scan as their next savior. It gives three handshakes with open ports and calls a method called connect () which makes the software to find TCP ports. sT scan when preferred can also be used to find UDP ports although people use it rarely.

Below is the command for -sT scan:

hacking @kali #nmap -sT 292.232.2.1

3) sU scan (UDP scan)

This scanning is also in the penetration-testing checklist after the importance of -sS scan. There is no need to send SYN packets like in TCP scan because this will just find UDP ports that are open. When the hackers start using the scan A UDP packet reaches the target host and waits for a positive response. If at all a response is received an open port is found. If it sends an error message with an Echo command then the port is closed.

Below is the command line for -sU scan

hacking @ kali #nmap -sU 292.232.2.1

4) sF scan (FIN scan)

This is a special type of scan that is used because some targets may have installed intrusion detection systems and firewalls that stop SYN packets that are sent using a TCP scan. For this sole reason, Fin scan is used if there is any extra detection scan happening on the other side. Fin scan does not save any log information to be detected so there is a great chance of the Fin packet to find out few open ports by sneaking into the target systems.

Here is the command for -sF scan

hacking@kali #nmap -sF 292.232.2.1

5) sP scan (Ping scan)

Ping is a famous network protocol method that checks whether a host is live or not by trying to connect to the target host. Ping scanning in Nmap also is used for the same purpose and is not used to check open ports. Ping scan asks for root access to start a scan. If you are not ready to provide the administrative privileges you can just use the connect method to start a ping sweep from Nmap.

Here is the command for -sP scan

hacking @ kali #nmap -sP 292.232.2.1

6) sV scan (version detection scan)

A version detection scan is one of the obsessive usages of Nmap for hackers. To attack a target system, you need to know about the technology and operating system the host is using so you create your exploits and backdoor strategies to break into the system. However, unlike TCP scans version detection scan takes a lot of time because when we start a sV scan in the background TCP scan gets started and searches for the open ports. After the hunt for open ports gets finished sV scan automatically analyzes them and determines the information about the target host. Due to this complex procedure, it may take a lot of time.

Here is the command for -sV scan

hacking @ kali #nmap -sV 292.232.2.1

7) sL scan (Idle scan)

This is one of the craziest features of Nmap because it just acts like a proxy server while doing attacks. When using idle scan you can send packets using another host Ip. This anonymity can help hackers to stay in the dark if something goes wrong or severe. Protecting himself from the investigation is what every hacker strives for especially in these modern times.

Here is the command for -sL scan

hacking @ kali #nmap -sL 292.432.2.6 292.432.2.1

Things Nmap can detect:

Nmap can detect the Device type of the host that is (router, workgroup, etc.), running operating system, operating system details i.e. version and network distance (approximate distance between the target and the attacker).

While using Nmap always use ping scan only when necessary because some firewalls in the target hosts can detect that an attack is going to happen and will block the attacker's addresses to make any connection.

By using the below command you are saying to the software that doesn't ping the remote host:

hacking @ kali # nmap -O -PN 292.428.5.6/ 12

Using the-PN parameter can bypass the Ping Command, but it does not affect the discovery of the host system. NMAP operating system detection is based on open and closed ports. If Os scan cannot detect at least one open or closed port, it will return the following error.

The error code is below:

Warning: we cannot find any open or closed ports to get information on the target system

It is difficult to accurately detect the remote operating system with NMAP, so we need to use NMAP's guess function, osscan-guess operation guesses which operating system type is closest to the target.

#nmap -O -osscan -guess 192.232.2.1

Before going to talk about Nessus let us have a simple exercise. Please try to do this Exercise for better understanding of the Information Gathering.

Exercise:

Start kali Linux terminal and enter into Nmap using the commands. Find the subnet masks for www.nmap.com and find the operating system and version that it uses. Complete different scans and create a detailed report on all the ports that are available.

Chapter 1 How to Setup and Install Kali Linux a USB Key

Kali Linux is the best hacking tool out there. It is super secure, and it is made by seasoned professionals who know what they are doing. What's so great about this system is that you can run it from a USB key and not have to worry about compromising or altering your current operating system. When you carry this OS on a USB key, it can be taken to any computer or compatible device and made to work. It only temporarily overrides the current operating system on that device.

Once you take out your USB key, you remove Kali Linux from the device. It doesn't leave behind any trace, and it doesn't change the settings or operating system of the device you used it on. It is compatible with any operating system because it works around them.

This is considered a non-destructive way to use Kali Linux. It lets everything go back to normal on whatever device you use it on, making no changes to the host's system. It's also portable, so you can take it from one workstation to the next and from one device to the next and do what you need to do. It starts up very fast, usually in just a few minutes, on whatever system you put it into.

You can also customize your bootable drive, using a Kali Linux ISO image that you rolled yourself. It is also potentially persistent. This means that, once you perform the proper configurations, your Kali Linux Live drive will keep the data it has collected no matter how many times you reboot it.

Installing onto Your Bootable USB Key

For Windows users, you will have to first download the Win32 Disk Imager utility. You'll find that <u>here</u>.

https://launchpad.net/win32-image-writer

If you are using a Linux or an OS X, just use the dd command. This has already been installed on both of th§ose platforms.

We recommend using a 4GB USB thumb drive or larger. If you want to use an SD card, then that's fine, since the procedure is the same for both. Just make sure the devices you are going to be using it on are compatible with your storage device.

The method for doing this will differ depending on what OS you have. We'll break it down on both of the major ones for you.

For Windows

Start by plugging your USB drive into a USB port on a PC operating Windows. Pay attention to the drive designator that it uses when it starts to mount. That designator will look like "F:\". Then launch the Win32 Disk Imager software. Once you open that software, pick out the Kali Linux ISO file you downloaded. Then click "Write" to copy it onto the USB drive, be sure you pick the right drive for this operation.

When the imaging process is finished, you can take out your USB. On most Windows OS, you will need to click on the small arrow near the bottom right corner of your screen to open a tab that shows connected devices. Be sure to click on your USB drive there to safely eject it and ensure that no information is lost when you disconnect it.

Once all that is done, you can boot Kali Linux from your USB device.

For Linux

Doing the same thing on a Linux is equally easy. Start with the verified ISO image and copy it over to the drive using the dd command. You have to be running as a root for this to work. Alternatively, you can execute the dd command using sudo. The instructions we're going to give you assume that you have a Linux Mint 17.1 desktop. Other versions are going to vary slightly, but the basic operations required for this task should all be about the same.

Just a word of warning before we get into the actual instruction: if you aren't sure what you are doing with dd command or you just aren't careful, you can accidently overwrite something you aren't meaning to. Be sure to double check everything you are doing so you don't make any mistakes.

Start by identifying the device path you are going to use to write the image onto the USB drive. Before the drive is inserted, perform the command "sudo fdisk -1"

You have to be using elevated privileges with fdisk, otherwise there won't be any output. Enter the above command in a terminal window at a command prompt. If you did it properly, you should see a single drive. That will probably look like this "/dev/sda". That drive will be separated into three partitions. These are /dev/sda1, /dev/sda2, and /dev/sda5.

From there, plug in the USB drive, then run the original command again. That's sudo fdisk -1. Once you do that, you will see another device that wasn't there initially. It could look something like this: "/dev/sdb".

Then take the ISO file and image it onto the USB device. It may take 10-15 minutes to image the USB device, so be patient. In order to perform this process, you need to execute the command below:

dd if=kali-linux-1.0.9a-amd32.iso of=/dev/sdb bs=512k

Let's dissect this command for a second. In the example we are using here, the ISO image that you want to write onto the drive is named "kali-linux-1.0.9a-amd32.iso". Yours may look slightly different. Note the "32" in the name. This refers to the size of the image. We use the blocksize value "bs=512k" because it is safe and reliable. You can make it bigger if you want, but that can cause some problems, so it isn't recommended.

Once the command is completed, then it will provide feedback and not before then. Your drive could have an access indicator. If it does, then it will blink every so often. How long this whole process takes will depend on a few factors- how fast your system is, what kind of USB drive you are using and how well your USB port works. The output, once the imaging is complete, will tell you how many bytes are copied and give you numbers for records in and out, which should be the same number.

Now your USB is ready to boot into a Kali Live environment.

Chapter 2 Darknet Markets

Just how safe is a Darknet in light of the vulnerabilities discussed? The short answer is, *as safe as you make it.*

You are the weak link. The last link in the security chain. And although you need Tor to access Onion sites, the term can apply to any anonymous network - networks like I2P or Freenet or anything else that cloaks the source of data transmit, and by extension, your identity.

Which brings us to the *Darknet Marketplace*.

The complete list of such marketplaces on the deep web are numerous, and the risk of getting scammed is quite high. It's one reason why you may not have heard about them. They are often taken down quickly by either a venomous reputation or a law enforcement bust. Sometimes they piss off the wrong people and then spammers ddos the site. But there are numerous places one can go if you're curious about what is sold by whom.

When I say *sold*, what I mean is, anything you want that cannot be gained through the usual legal channels. And remember that what is legal in one country may be illegal in another. In Canada, lolicon comics are illegal and can get you in big trouble if you cross the border. But not in America. In the USA you can pretty much write any story you want. In Canada? TEXT stories involving minors are verboten.

The other difference is that there are safety nets in buying almost anything in a first world country on the open market. Think BestBuy. Mom and Pop stores. Florist shops. If customers get injured, what happens? Customers sue via the legal safety net and make a lot of lawyers a lot of money.

But the Darknet Marketplace laughs at any such safety nets. In fact, you're likely to get scammed at least a few times before finding a reputable dealer for whatever goods you seek. And it really doesn't matter what it is, either - Teleportation devices? Pets? Exotic trees? It's all the same that goes around. Whatever is in demand will attract unsavory types and not just on the buyer's end.

Therefore, research any darknet market with Tor, being careful to visit forums and check updated information to see if any sites have been flagged as suspicious or compromised. Some other advice:

- Always use PGP to communicate.

- Never store crypto-currency at any such marketplace.

- Assume a den of thieves unless proven otherwise by *them*. The responsibility is theirs just as it is offline, to prove they are an honest business. If you open your own, keep this in mind: customers owe you nothing. You can only betray them once.

Now for some examples of Phishers and Scammers and other Con men. By their fruits, ye shall know them.

1.) <u>SILK ROAD 2.0</u> *(e5wvymnx6bx5euvy...)* Lots of scams with this one. Much like Facebook and Google emails, you can tell a fake sometimes by the address. Paste the first few letters into a shortcut next to the name. If it doesn't match, steer clear.

2.) **Green Notes Counter** (67yjqewxrd2ewbtp...) They promised counterfeit money to their customers but refuse escrow. A dead giveaway.

3.) iPhones for half off: (IPHONEAVZHWKQMAP...)

Now here is a prime example of a scam. Any website which sells electronic gadgets on the deep web is ripe for scamming customers. Whereas in the Far East you will merely get counterfeit phones with cheap, Chinese made parts that break within a month, on the Deep Web they will simply take your money and say adios. Actually, they won't even bother saying that.

So then, how does one tell a scam?

Because many new darknet vendors will arise out of thin air, with rare products that will make customers swoon and send them money - without doing any research on their name or previous sales. A real hit and run operation. Hit quick and fast and dirty. Seduce as many as they can before the herd catches on to the wolf in disguise. Many are suckered, thinking "it's only a little money, but a little money from a lot of Tor users goes a long way in encouraging other scammers to set up shop.

When you ask them why they do not offer escrow, they say "We think it is unreliable/suspicious/unstable" amid other BS excuses. It is better to hold on to your small change than leave a trail to your treasure chest. And make no mistake some of these scammers are like bloodhounds where identity theft is concerned.

Do your research! Check forums and especially the dates of reviews they have. Do you notice patterns? Are good reviews scattered over a long period of time or is it rather all of a sudden--the way some Amazon affiliate marketers do with paid reviews that glow? Not many reviews from said customers?

If you've seen the movie "Heat," with Al Pacino and Robert de Niro, you know when it is time to Walk Away.

In the middle of a nighttime heist, Niro goes outside for a smoke. He hears a distant cough. Somewhere. Now, this is middle of the night in an unpopulated part of the city that comes from across the street - a parking lot full of what he thought were empty trailers. Hmm, he thinks maybe this isn't such a great night for a hot score. Not so empty (it was a cop in a trailer full of other hotshot cops). He walks back into the bank and tells his partner to abort.

The other aspect is time. Some fake sites will set a short ship time and count on you not bothering to see the sale as finalized before you can whistle Dixie out of your ass. After finalization, you're screwed since the money is in their wallet before you can even mount a protest.

Fraud Prevention

One is Google believe it or not, at

http://www.google.com/imghp.

Dating sites like Cherry Blossoms and Cupid sometimes use reverse image search to catch fakers and Nigerian scammers masquerading as poor lonely singles to deprive men of their coinage. If they can catch them, so can you. If the image belongs to some other legit site, chances are it is fake. **Foto Forensics** also does the same, and reports metadata so that it becomes even harder to get away with Photoshop trickery.

<u>When it is Okay to FE (Finalize Early)</u>

FE means 'Finalize Early'. It's use online can usually be found in black marketplaces like Silk Road and Sheep's Marketplace. It simply means that money in escrow is released before you receive your product. Every customer I've ever spoken with advises against this unless you've had great experience with that business.

But... quite a few vendors are now making it a *standard practice* to pay funds up front before you have anything in your hands.

On more than one Marketplace forum, there's been heated exchange as to when this is proper. You might hear, "Is this guy legit? What about this Chinese outfit over here? He seems shady," and others: "A friend said this guy is okay but then I got ripped off!". You get the idea.

Here is my experience on the matter.

1.) It is okay when you are content with not getting what you paid for. This may seem counterproductive, but think how many gamblers go into a Las Vegas casino and never ask themselves "How much can I afford to lose?"

The answer, sadly, is not many. Vegas was not built on the backs of losers. Some merchants do not like escrow at all. Some do. So don't spend more than you can afford to lose. Look at it the way a gambler looks at making money.

2.) It is okay when you are guaranteed shipment. There are FE scammers out there that will give you an angelic smile and lie right into your eyes as they swindle you. Do not depend solely on reviews. A guy on SR can be the best merchant this side of Tatooine and yet you will wake up one day and find yourself robbed. He's split with a million in BTC and you're left not even holding a bag. Most won't do this to you. But a few will.

When it is NOT Okay to FE

When losing your funds will result in you being evicted or a relationship severed. Never borrow money from friends and especially not family unless you want said family to come after you with a double-bladed ax. If you get ripped off, you lose not only the cash but the respect and trustworthiness of your family. Word spreads. You don't pay your debts. What's that saying in Game of Thrones?

Right. A Lannister always pays his debts. So should you.

MultiSigna

Sounds like something from Battlestar Galactica to pass from ship to ship. A badge of honor perhaps some hotshot flyboy wears on his fighter jacket that bypassed a lot of red tape.

While not exactly mandatory, it makes for interesting reading, and is something Tor users might want to know about if they wish to make purchases anonymously. Here's what happens:

When a purchase is enacted, the seller deposits money (in this case, Bitcoins) in a multi-signature address. After this, the customer gets notification to make the transaction ($,€) to the seller's account.

Then after the seller relays to MultiSigna that the transaction was a success, MultiSigna creates a transaction from the multi-signature address that requires both buyer and seller so that it may be sent to the network. The buyer gets the Bitcoins and ends the sale. Confused yet? I was too at first. You'll get used to it.

Critical

MultiSigna only exists as a verifier/cosigner of the entire transaction. If there is disagreement between seller and buyer, NO EXCHANGE occurs. Remember the scene in Wargames when two nuclear silo operators have to turn their keys simultaneously in order to launch? Yeah, that.

MultiSigna will of course favor one or the other, but not both if they cannot mutually agree. The upside is that is if the market or purchaser or vendor loses a key, two out of three is still available. A single key cannot spend the money in 2/3 MultiSig address.

Is it Safe? Is it Secret?

I don't recommend enacting a million dollar exchange for a yacht, or even a thousand dollar one as they both carry risk, but ultimately it is up to you. Just remember that trust is always an issue on darknets, and you're generally safer making several transfers with a seller/buyer who has a good history of payment. In other words, reputation as always, is everything.

Alas, there are a few trustworthy markets that have good histories of doing things properly, thank heavens.

Blackbank is one. **Agora** is another. Take a look at the Multi-Sig Escrow Onion page here with Tor:

http://u5z75duioy7kpwun.onion/wiki/index.php/Multi-Sig_Escrow

Security

What the effect would be if a hacker gained entry to the server? What mischief might he make? What chaos could he brew if he can mimic running a withdrawal in the same manner that the server does?

If a hacker were to gain access and attempt to withdraw money, a single-signature would be applied and passed to the second sig signer for co-signature. Then the security protocol would kick in where these policies would be enforced:

1.) Rate limits: the rate of stolen funds slows

2.) Callbacks to the spender's server: Signing service verifies with the original spender that they initiated and intended to make the spend. The callback could go to a separated machine, which could only contain access to isolated approved withdrawal information.

3.) IP limiting: The signing service only signs transactions coming from a certain list of IPs, preventing the case where the hacker or insider stole the private key.

4.) Destination Whitelists: Certain very high security wallets can be set such that the signing service would only accept if the destination were previously known.

The hacker would have to compromise both the original sending server as well as the signing service.

Let me repeat that MultiSigna are *never in possession* of your bitcoins. They use 2 of 3 signatures (seller, buyer & MultiSigma) to sign a transaction. Normal transactions are signed by the seller and then by the buyer.

Purchaser Steps for MultiSig Escrow

1.) Deposit your Bitcoins. Purchase ability is granted after 6 confirmations

2.) Make a private & public key (Brainwallet.org is a JavaScript Client-Side Bitcoin Address Generator)

3.) Buy item, input public-key & a refund BTC address

4.) Retrieve purchased item

5.) Input the private key and close

Chapter 3 Web Security

In this chapter, we will briefly talk about web security and about some attacks that you need to have in mind. I'm absolutely sure you've heard a lot of times on TV, radio or from other sources of the company's X site being broken, the organization's Y site being down and hackers replacing the main site with a fake page.

Well, I want to tell you that at large (Less Experienced Hackers) they all look for many vulnerabilities well known to their sites 1 to 2 that they can take advantage of. There are many tools that help them locate these vulnerabilities relatively easily, and then help them exploit them.

Some of these vulnerabilities (web-level) are extremely well presented and documented in the Open Web Application Security Project (*OWASP*). OWASP is a nonprofit organization dedicated to improving the security of software and web applications.

They have a *top 10* with the most commonly reported security incidents in previous years on websites and web applications. OWASP organizes even local events (you can research on Google or Facebook for such events), creating a community of passionate cyber security people.

If you hear at some point of such an event and you have the opportunity to go, I recommend you to take this step because you will see that it is worthwhile first and secondly that you learn a lot of things from many people.

As you can see for the most part, it's about the same type of vulnerabilities, with the top changing very little over a three-year period. We will only take some of these attacks and explain to you what each person represents and how you can do them on your own site.

Here are the attacks, we will discuss further:

- SQL injection

- **XSS**

- Security Misconfiguration

Now let's start talking about web attacks with the first attack / vulnerability (and most common) from the list above:

1) SQL Injection

When we talk about SQL injection, we are talking primarily about databases, and secondly about the attack (a vulnerability) at their level. Let's first look at what SQL is. *SQL* (*Structured Query Language*) is a query language with databases. It is used to communicate directly with the database through various commands addressed to it. There are several types / forms of SQL, but the basics are the same.

Where are the SQL injection attacks? Most often these occur when the attacker finds a "box" in which he can enter data. For example, think about a search box in which anyone can write anything.

If the back code (most often PHP) is not written properly, then the hacker can enter SQL commands that interact directly with the database, so they can extract different information.

Now I want you to think that when you interact with an "input form" (a box where you can write and send something to the server), this happens:

████████████████████████████████

That is, PHP language will generate such an order to interact (and search) with the database. In the place where '%' appears, it will be replaced with what you enter in that input form.

Here's an example of a SQL code that can be entered in this field (ATTENTION: it will not work for any site. I suggest using the bWAPP application and testing it):

```
' OR 1=1;--
```

You can try on **this site** (https://sqlzoo.net/hack/) to enter the SQL statement above instead of the username and password.

SQLmap (http://sqlmap.org/) is a great tool you can use to *test database vulnerabilities* on a site. SQLmap will do all these queries that automatically automate SQL injection for you (and even try to break the hash of the passwords you will find in the database).

Another reason why WordPress is so used is due to the number of existing plugins that can be used to improve the site, user experience, etc. So the person who manages a site / blog using such a CMS does NOT need programming skills because the plugins deal (mostly) with everything that's needed. There are over 50,000 free plugins available in the WordPress marketplace, and besides these, the paid ones that have been developed by different companies.

Another very interesting aspect related to WordPress is that he is Open Source. This means it is developed by a community of programmers to whom anyone can take part.

As running technologies, WordPress needs *LAMP* (*Linux, Apache, MySQL, PHP*). Each of these components is critical in running a site. If you are not familiar with LAMP I will briefly explain what each component is:

1. *Linux* - The OS on which the site will work, the reason being simple: a flexible,
   stable OS and more secure than Windows
2. *Apache* - The web server used to host the site, most widespread in the Internet
3. *MySQL* - The database used by WordPress to store the information site (articles, users, comments and any other type of content that requires storage)
4. *PHP* - The programming language that interacts with each component (base data, web server and OS). PHP is a web programming language used on the backhand side (what we do not see when we access a site)

If you want to install WordPress for your own use, you will need a web hosting server. I recommend you USE

THIS ONE (BLUEHOST) - http://bit.ly/2HvO3je- (which provides you with 1-click install so you can start immediately using your WordPress site.

Now, after installing WordPress, I suggest we move on to a security scanning tool for your website.

WPScan

WPScan is a scan tool (and of course a crack) of a WordPress-based site. It is open source, so it can be used by anyone who wants to test their site for vulnerabilities. This tool can give you a lot of information about your site:

- The WordPress version used (a very good indicator)
- Plugins installed
- Potential vulnerabilities existing on the site, which can then be exploited
- Finding existing users on the site
- Making Brute Force attacks by using a password finder

Often, scanning can be perceived as actively testing your system to see what you can find through it. You can compare this concept to the one in which someone (stranger) wants to "see" what you have in the house. Enter the door (without you being home) and start looking through your things, but do not take anything in order to use that information later.

Makes a non-intrusive scan ():

wpscan --url www.example.com

Enumerates (lists) the installed plugins:

wpscan --url www.example.com --enumerate p

Runs all enumeration tools in order to learn as much information as possible:

wpscan --url www.example.com --enumerate

List the existing users on the site:

wpscan --url www.example.com --enumerate u

These are some ways to use the WPScan tool. In below, I placed my first order on a WordPress-based site (whose identity I will not publish) to see what information we can find out about it. I mention that I was authorized to do such a scan on this site.

And from a simple scan of how many vulnerabilities I found on this site (he definitely needs an update). As you see, there are many vulnerabilities that can be exploited using different methods. Moreover, there are also these **CVE**S (*Common Vulnerability and Exposures*) https://www.cvedetails.com/browse-by-date.php that describe the vulnerability and how it can be exploited.

Because we're talking about WordPress and *vulnerabilities* after all, **HERE** (https://wpvulndb.com/) you can see a database that contains all the *vulnerabilities known* and made *public* for each version. In addition to this, I want to tell you that all the attacks, we have talked about in this chapter also apply to the WordPress case. Unfortunately, *SQLi, XSS, Traversal Directory* are only a few (of many) attacks that can be done relatively easily on this platform. With WPScan all you do is find them much faster.

It's important *to be aware* of them, to frequently scan your website (yourself or a client), discover new vulnerabilities, and do them to resolve them as quickly as possible.

5) Google Hacking

I think you had a slightly different reaction when you saw the title of this topic: "Wow! can I hack up Google?" or "can I hack with Google?" I can tell you yes, in the 2nd situation (although the first is not excluded: D). You can use Google to discover different sites that have certain *pages indexed* in the search engine. Thus, using a few specific search keywords, Google can give you exactly what you are looking for (*sites* that contain exactly the *URL* you are looking for with a vulnerable plug-in, a database information page like that be the user, the password and the name of the database, etc.).

Yes, site administrators are not mindful (probably not even aware) of their site being able to *leak valuable information on Google*, making it extremely exposed to Internet attacks.

Again, I give you this information because you can use it for ethical purposes (to research and test your site or that of a customer). Do not forget that unauthorized access to a system will be penalized and you may take a few years in prison for this (I know a few people who have suffered this ...).

Now that you have remembered this, here are some examples where you can do a research. With this search, Google will display sites that have a WordFence plugin (a site security plug-in - firewall, virus scanner, etc.)

inurl:"/wp-content/plugins/wordfence/"
This was just one example (in). Of course you can replace search content by "*inurl:*" with whatever you want, depending on your current interest.

By following the order in Google Search, you will be able to see different sites depending on the version of WordPress they use. Then you can use WPScan and find out more about the vulnerabilities that exist on it, then you can try to take advantage of it (ethically). You will see that there are many very old, extremely vulnerable versions of WordPress. What I recommend you is to get in touch with the site admin, to make him aware that he is exposed to a massive risk and to ask him to let you prove it (that is, attacking his site) : D).

inurl:"wordpress readme.html"

Chapter 4 Information Gathering Tools

The beginning of any attacks initiates from the stage of information gathering. When you gather as much information about the target, the attack becomes an easy process. Having information about the target also results in a higher success rate of the attack. A hacker finds all kinds of information to be helpful.

The process of information gathering includes:

1. Gathering information that will help in social engineering and ultimately in the attack
2. Understanding the range of the network and computers that will be the targets of the attack
3. Identifying and understanding all the complete surface of the attack i.e. processes and systems that are exposed
4. Identifying the services of a system that are exposed, and collecting as much information about them as possible
5. **Querying specific service that will help fetch useful data such as usernames**

We will now go through Information Gathering tools available in Kali Linux one by one.

Nmap and Zenman

Ethical hacking is a phase in Kali Linux for which the tools NMap and ZenMap are used. NMap and ZenMap are basically the same tool. ZenMap is a Graphical Interface for the NMap tool which works on the command line.

The NMap tool which is for security auditing and discovery of network is a free tool. Apart from penetration testers, it is also used by system administrators and network administrators for daily tasks such as monitoring the uptime of the server or a service and managing schedules for service upgrades.

NMap identifies available hosts on a network by using IP packets which are raw. This also helps NMap identify the service being hosted on the host which includes the name of the application and the version. Basically, the most important application it helps identify on a network is the filter or the firewall set up on a host.

Stealth Scan

The Stealth scan is also popularly known as the hal open scan or SYN. It is called the half open scan because it refrains from completing the usual three-way handshake of TCP. So how it works is a SYN packet is sent by an attacker to the target host. The target host will acknowledge the SYN and sent a SYN/ACK in return. If a SYN/ACK is received, it can be safely assumed that the connection to the target host will complete and the port is open and listening on the target host. If the response received is RST instead, it is safe to assume that the port is close or not active on the target host.

acccheck

The acccheck tool was developed has an attack tool consisting of a password dictionary to target Windows Authentication processes which use the SMB protocol. The accccheck is basically a wrapper script which is injected in the binary of 'smbclient' and therefore depends on the smbclient binary for execution.

Server Message Block (SMB) protocol is an implementation of Microsoft for file sharing over a network and is popularly known as the Microsoft SMB Protocol.

It was then extended to the SMB "Inter-Process Communication" (IPC) system which implements named pipes and was one of the first inter process services that programmers got access to and which served as a means of inheritance for multiple services for authentication as they would all use the same credentials as that which were keyed in for the very first connection to the SMB server.

Amap

Amap is a scanning too of the next generation that allows a good number of options and flags in its command line syntax making it possible to identify applications and processes even if the ports that they are running on are different.

For example, a web server by default accepts connections on port 80. But most companies may change this port to something else such as 1253 to make the server secure. This change would be easily discovered by Amap.

Furthermore, if the services or applications are not based on ASCII, Amap is still able to discover them. Amap also has a set of interesting tools, which have the ability to send customized packets which will generate specific responses from the target host.

Amap, unlike other network tools is not just a simple scanner, which was developed with the intention of just pinging a network to detect active hosts on the network. Amap is equipped with amapcrap, which is a module that sends bogus and completely random data to a port. The target port can be UDP, TCP, SSL, etc. The motive is to force the target port to generate a response.

CaseFile

A huge number of Maltegousers were using Maltego to try and build graphical data from offline investigations and that is how CaseFile was born. Since there was no need of the transform provided by Maltego and the real need was just the graphing capability of Maltego in and more flexible way, CaseFile was developed.

CaseFile, being an application of visual intelligence, helps to determine the relationships, connections and links in the real world between information of different types. CaseFile lets you understand the connections between data that may apart from each other by multiple degrees of separation by plotting the relationships between them graphically. Additionally, CaseFile comes bundled with many more entities that are useful in investigations making it a tool that is efficient. You can also add your custom entities to CaseFile, which allows you to extend this tool to your own custom data sets.

braa

Braa is a tool that is used for scanning mass Simple Network Management Protocol (SNMP). The tool lets you make SNMP queries, but unlike other tools which make single queries at a time to the SNMP service, braa has the capability to make queries to multiple hosts simultaneously, using one single process. The advantage of braa is that it scans multiple hosts very fast and that too by using very limited system resources.

Unlike other SNMP tools, which require libraries from SNMP to function, braa implements and maintains its own stack of SNMP. The implementation is very complex and dirty. Supports limited data types, and cannot be called up to standard in any case. However braa was developed to be a fast tool and it is fast indeed.

dnsmap

dnsmap is a tool that came into existence originally in 2006 after being inspired from the fictional story "The Thief No One Saw" by Paul Craig.

A tool used by penetration testers in the information gathering stage, dnsmap helps discover the IP of the target company, domain names, netblocks, phone numbers, etc.

Dnsmap also helps on subdomain brute forcing which helps in cases where zone transfers of DNS do not work. Zone transfers are not allowed publicly anymore nowadays which makes dnsmap the need of the hour.

DotDotPwn

The dotdotpwn tool can be defined simply to call it a fuzzer. What is a fuzzer? A fuzzer is a testing tool that targets software for vulnerabilities by debugging and penetrating through it. It scans the code and looks for flaws and loopholes, bad data, validation errors, parameters that may be incorrect and other anomalies of programming.

Whenever an anomaly is encountered by the software, the software may become unresponsive, making way for the flaws to give an open door to an attack. For example, if you are an attacker whose target is a company's web server, with the help of dotdotpwn, you will be able to find a loophole in the code of the web server. Perhaps there has been a latest HTTP update on the server overnight. Using a fuzzer on the web server shows you there is an exploit with respect to data validation which leaves an open door for a DoS attack. You can now exploit this vulnerability, which will make the server crash and server access will be denied to genuine employees of the company. There are many such errors that can be discovered using a fuzzer and it is very common for technology to have error when it releases something new in the market and it takes time to identify the error and fix it.

Another example would be an attack with respect to SQL called SQLi where 'i' stands for injection. SQL injection attacks are achieved by injecting SQL database queries through web forms that are available on a website. The conclusion is that software will always be vulnerable allowing attackers to find a way to break their way into the system.

Fierce

Fierce is a Kali tool which is used to scan ports and map networks. Discovery of hostnames across multiple networks and scanning of IP spaces that are non-contiguous can be achieved by using Fierce. It is a tool much like Nmap but in case of Fierce, it is used specifically for networks within a corporate.

Once the target network has been defined by a penetration tester, Fierce runs a whole lot of tests on the domains in the target network and retrieves information that is valuable and which can be analyzed and exploited by the attacker.

Fierce has the following features.

- Capabilities for a brute-force attack through custom and built-in test list

- Discovery of nameservers

- Zone transfer attacks

- Scan through IP ranges both internal and external

- Ability to modify the DNS server for reverse host lookups

Wireshark

Wireshark is a kali too that is an open source analyzer for network and works on multiple platforms such as Linux, BSD, OS X and Windows.

It helps one understand about the functioning of a network thus making it of use in government infrastructure, education industries and other corporates.

It is similar to the tcpdump tool, but WIreshark is a notch above as it has a graphical interface through which you can filter and organize the data that has been captured, which means that it takes less time to analyze the data further. There is also an only text based version known as tshark, which has almost the same amount of features.

Wireshark has the following features.

- The interface has a user-friendly GUI

- Live capture of packets and offline analysis

- Support for Gzip compression and extraction

- Inspection of full protocol

- Complete VOiP analysis

- Supports decryption for IPsec, Kerberos, SSL/TLS, WPA/WPA2

URLCrazy

URLCrazy is a Kali tool that can that tests and generates typos and variations in domains to target and perform URL hijacking, typo squatting and corporate espionage. It has a database that can generate variants of up to 15 types for domains, and misspellings of up to 8000 common spellings. URLCrazy supports a variety of keyboard layouts, checks if a particular domain is in use and figures how popular a typo is.

The Harvester

The Harvester is a Kali tool that is not your regular hacking tool. Whenever there is a mention of hacking tools that are implemented using the command line, one usually thinks of tools like Nmap, Reaver, Metasploit and other utilities for wireless password cracking. However, the harvester refrains from using algorithms that are advanced to break into firewalls, or crack passwords, or capture the data of the local network.

Instead, the Harvester simply gathers publicly available information such as employee names, email addresses, banners, subdomains and other information in the same range. You may wonder as to why it collects this data. Because this data is very useful in the primary stage of information gathering. All this data helps study and understand the target system which makes attacking easier for the hacker or the penetration tester.

Furthermore, it helps the attacker understand as to how big and Internet footprint the target has. It also helps organizations to know how much publicly available information their employees have across the Internet. The latest version of the Harvester has updates which lets it keep intervals between the requests it makes to pages on the Internet, improves search sources, plotting of graphs and statistics, etc.

The Harvester crawls through the Internet as your surrogate, looking for information on your behalf as long as the criteria provided by you matches the information on the Internet. Given that you can also gather email addresses using the Harvester, this tool can be very useful to a hacker who is trying to penetrate an online login by gaining access to the email account of an individual.

Metagoofil

Metagoofil is a kali tool that is aimed at fetching publicly available such as pdf, xls, doc, ppt, etc. documents of a company on the Internet.

The tool makes a Google search to scan through documents and download them to the local machine. It then extracts the metadata of the documents using libraries such as pdfminer, hachoir, etc. It then feeds the information gathering process with the results of its report which contains usernames, server or machine names and software version which helps penetration testers with their investigation.

Miranda

Miranda is a Kali tool that is actively or passively used to detect UPnP hosts, its services, its devices and actions, all through on single command. The Service state parameters and their associated actions are correlated automatically and are then processed as input/output variables for every action. Miranda uses a single data structure to store information of all the hosts and allows you access to that data structure and all its contents.

Let's discuss what exactly ÚPnP is. Universal Plug and Play or UPnP is a protocol for networking that allows devices on the network such as computers, printers, routers mobile devices, etc. to discover each other seamlessly over a network and established services between them for sharing of data, entertainment and other communication. It is ideally for networks inside a private residence as opposed to corporate infrastructure.

Ghost Phisher

Ghost Phisher is a Kali tool, which is used as an attack software program and also for security auditing of wired and wireless networks. It is developed using the Python programming language and the Python GUI library. The program basically emulates access points of a network therefore, deploying its own internal server into a network.

Fragroute

Fragroute is a Kali tool that is used for intercepting, modifying and rewriting traffic that is moving toward a specific host. Simply put, the packets from attacking system known as frag route packets are routed to the destination system. It is used for bypassing firewalls mostly by attackers and security personnel. Information gathering is a well-known use case for fragroute as well which used by penetration testers who use a remote host, which is highly secured.

Masscan

Masscan is a Kali tool, which is used by penetration testers all around the world and has been in the industry for a long time. It is a tool of reconnaissance which has the capability to transmit up to 10 million packets every second. The transmission used by masscan is asynchronous and it has custom stack of TCP/IP. Therefore, the threads used for sending and receiving packets are unique.

Masscan is used to simultaneously attack a large number of hosts and that too quickly. The tool developer claims that masscan can scan the entire Internet in 6 minutes. Given its super high transmission rate, it has a use case in the domain of stress testing as well.

However, to achieve those high transmission rates, special drives and NICs are required. The communication of the tool with the users is very similar to that between the user and the Nmap tool.

Feature of masscan are as follows.

- It can be used to enumerate the whole Internet

- It can be used to enumerate a huge number of hosts

- Various subnets within an organization can be enumerated

- It can be used for random scanning and fun on the Internet

Chapter 5 Advanced Kali Linux Concepts

Using abusive services

Services are the most important mechanisms that Linux operates for a better functioning of the operating system. Even windows have services that run-in background. Basically, services are processes that run in the background until you use it. For example, consider a proxy server like Burp suite that will intercept every information that goes on in the browser and if you click No it stops the service and nothing goes there. In windows, which is quite well dominated by graphical user, interfaces services are easily closed down by a click. Whereas in Linux we need to start using command line to start, stop and restart services.

Why services matter to hackers?
Hackers should be well learnt about services because when you are trying to exploit a system you need to stop services that can interrupt what you are doing. Clever administrators use services to make hackers confuse. So, you need to understand the services that are making your exploitation difficult and stop them as soon as

possible. Some advanced hackers install their own services after exploiting the system in a way that they will receive valuable information from the host regularly. In the below section we will explain with command line examples that will help us understand dealing with services.

1) Starting a Service

To start burp suite as a service go to Linux terminal as a root user and just use the following command.

root @ kali:service burpsuite start

This will start the service and you can check it using the ps command.

2) Stopping a Service

Stopping a service will completely abort everything that service is dealing with. So always, be careful while stopping a service as any unsaved data will be lost. Now use the following command to stop the service.

root @ kali:service burpsuite stop

You can check using ps command where you will not see anything related to burpsuit service.

3) Restarting a Service

Restarting a service just reboots everything about a particular service. Data will be lost and new service arises all on its own.

root @ kali:service burpsuit restart

This can be used when any service is struck or stops abruptly.

Now in this below section we will use the Apache web server and MySQL to explain how services can be useful for a hacker. This is a very basic and introductory level of abusing services. If you are an efficient hacker, you will understand hundreds of services and will try to learn about them in time and time to be a professional. Now let us start exploring these below services.

1) Apache Web server:

Apache is a famous web server that is being used by several hosting companies for deploying their web services. It is a well known open source web server that is well structured and of good security. We will use this apache web server to learn a few things that can help us as a hacker.

Step 1: Starting Apache

Apache webserver can be started using the following command. Normally in windows and Hosting environment there will be a GUI that lets us start the Apache web server. But in Linux we need to enter the following command as a root user.

root @ kali: service apache start

This will start the web server in the background, which can be accessed from the localhost. You can check if everything is going well or not using ps command.

Step 2: Accessing the local host

Now after starting the server you can go to your local host address that is http://127.0.0.1 using your browser to access apache. You will be welcomed with an apache page that asks your permission to show the default page.

Step 3: Modify the webpage

Now for a practical example, modify html file to your desired and save it using any text editor. After few seconds come back to localhost and refresh. Boom! You can see the modified webpage. This confirms that service is being run on the background.

How an apache web server can help hackers? Programmers to create a local host website during development phase usually use Apache web server. This can be linked with WAMP to further expand it with Php or MySQL servers. However, hackers can use it to learn about loopholes in websites without being blocked or banned. Hackers can also use Apache web server applications like Vulnerable App to expand their hacking skills. Almost every Hackathon program use the Apache web server for making their Hacking boxes.

Logging system

Being a hacker, you will certainly visit networks with high-level protection and maintained by hardworking security engineers. And if with all your skills you have exploited the system. After the attack, obviously a forensic investigation will take place and will try to find how an attack has been planned and executed. Everything of this investigation will be based on logfiles that you have left while exploiting the system.

Linux unlike windows is not vulnerable to exploits and attacking's because it has good logging system that records everything the user does. But some smart hackers use different techniques to make themselves undetectable by reading logfiles. We will explain in detail about how hackers need to develop skills to manipulate the logging system.

rsyslog

rsyslog is a definite daemon program that takes care of log files to be created in the UNIX or Linux system. Every Linux distribution uses different techniques to deploy log files. Arch Linux uses a different process unlike Debian rsyslog function. As we are discussing about kali Linux that is a Debian system we will continue with rsyslog explanation along with few examples.

kern.*   -var/log/kern.log

This is where log instructions are given to the Linux kernel. When we look at it thoroughly, we will find a basic command that log functionality uses. It is as the command shown below.

facility.priority action

We need to describe these three things in detail to get a thorough overview about the concept.

    1) Facility
Facility is something, which is being logged. For example, mail designates about the mail system. There are few that comes under this category as explained below.

a) mail

This explains about the mailing system that is present in kali Linux. This precisely says that mail usage is being logged

b) user

All user related instructions or functions comes under this category.

c) kern

All messages that deals with the kernel comes under this category

d) lpr

All messages that deals with the inbuilt printing system comes under this.

2) Priority

If the facility describes which messages to log, priority decides on what to log. There are different types of messages that can be used to a better logging system. We will describe some of them below.

a) debug

This is used to log the things that happen as it is.

b) warning

This is used to log things that work but can go wrong.

c) info

This is used to log about normal information that exists. This can also be used to log date and time.

d) error

This can be used if something badly goes wrong while doing a work in Linux.

3) Action

This is quite simple to understand than the rest. It just means that the logs should be sent into this particular category. We may manually assign folder but it's better to leave them, as it is to go to var folder for better management. We will give some example destinations that logs are sent normally

a) Kernel files:

These are normally sent to /var/log/kernel . You can just go to the directory and open the log file using leafpad to analyze them.

Now as we have learned everything we will just look at an example that deals with all of this.

mail.warning /var/log/warning

This precisely means that mail system warning message logs will be sent to /var/log/warning path.

Automatically clean logs

Log files can make up a lot of mess if you use them extensively. We need to make a strategy to keep how many logs depending on the time interval. However, we can use logrotate function in kali Linux to configure few functions that can help us clean log files.

Open logrotate.conf file and modify the text file to create your own log system according to your own necessity.

How to spoof log files?

You might wonder being a hacker how people get rid of tracking when they attack any target host. Luckily, Linux provides few functions, which can help us to spoof log files that is to modify them in a way such that network administrators cannot detect what happened during the attack. This process is called shred. We will explain about this process in detail in the below section.

Step 1:

Shred function just fills the log data with randomly generated UTF-8 code in the logged data again and again to make it as unusable data. To check shred function just click the below command in the Linux terminal as a root user.

root @ kali: shred

Step 2:

To make any file into unusable shred file you need to call the shred command with the file name. That's it. With a single click, all your data will be made into a difficult data that cannot be read or understood by anyone. The command is as below:

root @ kali: shred (insert file name here)

root @ kali: shred desktop/kalishred.txt

Step 3:

There is a special function in shred command that can help you shred the file as number of times you needed to be. But the only negative thing to worry about this is when you try to shred a file by 20 times the time taken will increase exponentially. So always listen to your senses when trying to shred a file multiple times. -n command describes the number of times function. Command is shown as below:

root @ kali : shred -n 20 /desktop/kalishred.txt

There is also another way to make logging stop. When you have control over system as a root user, you can simply disable the service by using the following command. We can use three commands start, stop and restart for this service.

a) start

This starts the logging function allover again.

root@kali: service rsyslog start

b) stop

This stops the logging function in a split of a second.

root@kali: service rsyslog stop

c) Restart

This will first stop the logging function and will start again as a new variable.

root@kali: service rsyslog restart

Automating tasks with job scheduling

As a hacker, the most important skill you need to learn is to automate things. Whenever you attack a system or exploit a system, you need to get ready with a ton of things that will automate things for you. An automated backup or automated deletion of logfiles everything needs to be done for a better productivity and results.

In this section, we will discuss in detail about automating tasks using kali Linux.

crontab

Crontab is a function that is available in kali Linux that will let us schedule an event or job for a particular time. We can enter the data from minutes to years to start a crontab task.

root @ kali : crontab

Click -help to check the functions of the crontab in detail.

Scheduling a backup task

Backup is one of the essential thing to do whenever you are dealing with an important data. When data is backed up, it can be used as an alternative if there is any leakage or corrupt in data. So administrators always prefer backing up the data. But it is a difficult and boring task to backup manually every day. So we can create an automatic backup with the following command.

00 1 18,28 ** backup/desktop/backup.sh

Here first 00 stands for the top of the hour. And ** to any day of the month.

Crontab shortcuts

Below we will display a few shortcuts that are used in crontab automatic task scheduling.

1) @yearly

This will make the task to run once a year.

2) @ weekly

This will make a task to run once in a week

3) @ midnight

This will make a task to run at midnight every day.

Starting tasks at startup with rc

While startup certain scripts start their tasks automatically using rc scripts. This will help them prioritize in the process and will give good results. If you are willing to add a service to start automatically on a startup, you can use the following command.

root @ kali : update-rc.d servicename enable/disable

Protecting you with TOR and VPN

It is obvious that the most important thing for any hacker is his anonymity. Now days due to restrictions of Government and constant spying had made people to find alternate options to maintain anonymity like TOR and VPN. Before going to learn how to maintain your anonymity in Kali Linux, we will have a good explanation about all the options we have for securing ourselves in this matrix world that is all connected.

Why Anonymity matters?

Imagine if your country has blocked your internet access to social networking during riots and all of your people want to use it for better communication. You can do with a VPN or TOR bundle and not are detected. However, tracking can be done in any other way if they want to. But make sure to follow this for some better peace. In the below section we will learn about anonymity services that has different uses.

What is a proxy server?

Proxy is a middle man between you and server that you are trying to reach. Imagine if you want to deliver a package from New York (your place) to Colorado (Server place). Instead of going and giving the package all by your own, you will ask your friend to deliver it. Here your friend acts a proxy for you. This is how the proxy server works.

There are many proxy servers like Socks4, http, https and Socks5.

How a hacker can use proxy server?

When doing a password attack you will normally be blocked by the website due to too many requests. In these situations, you can use a bunch of free proxies to randomly occupy the proxy address and attack the login page. This is a famous technique called cracking that is used by novice hackers to get an access into the system.

What is a VPN?

A VPN is a quite common advertisement that you might have used while watching ads in YouTube. A virtual private network abbreviated as a VPN acts like a middle man but delivers your request in encrypted form to the server in such a way that the server can't identify you. And when the server sends you the response it again encrypts it and sends towards you. Imagine this example to get a better understanding of how a Vpn works. Imagine that you want to deliver a Love Letter to your classmate. But you don't want any other person to read it other than your best friend. So, you write a Letter in quite a different way that no one can understand and sends by your friend to your classmate. Remember that your friends know how to read it. He will decrypt it to her and she will send a response in the same way. This is basically how a VPN works.

In the next section, we will describe about how internet communication works and will give a practical example that will let us understand the fact that Anonymity is a must.

How the internet works?

Every internet connected device has an IP address that can be easily tracked using different techniques by the government. When u send an email or surf internet without any Anonymity services, you are just being a product to Tech giants like Google. They will collect a lot of information from you and will sell you as adds to the businesses. Apart from that, every movement of yours will be tracked and can help them create new products.

Normally when we click on an URL the packet that contains your request will also contain the IP addresses of both yours and the server that you are trying to reach. In the communication process, it will travel through different routers called hops before reaching its final destination. When a packet is travelling, it can be easily sniffed and can be used to acquire information about you.

For an example, use traceroute command to check how many hops that a particular website takes as below.

root @ kali: traceroute bing.com

You will get an output that shows the number of routers it needs to travel to reach the final destination. When the packet is travelling, anyone can sniff it and can attain sensitive information about you and your request.

Chapter 6 Bash Scripting and Python Scripting

What is bash Scripting? A shell script is basically a text file that contains containing a string of commands in sequence. When the script is run, it executes all the commands that are in the file. The "shell" in the phrase refers to the command-line user interface that is used to communicate with the Linux kernel. There are a few different shells currently in use, with the most common ones being the C shell or csh, the Korn shell or ksh, the Bourne shell or sh, and the Bourne-Again shell or bash.

There are a number of scenarios that will require you to script with the shell. You may for instance have to support existing scripts, or you may wish to automate the system setup procedure before installing Oracle. In this scenario, you may use a script to determine the state of the operating system and any system requirements that you will have to meet before the software can be installed.

Linux

The most commonly used shell under Linux is called "Bash". This name is derived from "Bourne Again Shell". Although there are many other types of shells available for Linux, most experts recommend that you stick to the Bash shell, since this will increase the portability of your scripts between different systems and operating systems.

UNIX

Under UNIX, the shell allows a programmer to string together and execute a number of UNIX commands without having to compile them first. This makes it a lot faster to get a script running. In addition, shell scripting under UNIX makes it easier for other programmers to read and understand your code. Such shell scripts are also usually easily portable across the entire UNIX world, as long as they conform to a set standard.

Scripting for Windows

The Windows operating system conveniently includes a basic command structure that can be used to create scripts that will essentially streamline various administrative tasks. Some of the more common scripting languages under the Windows platform are Windows shell scripting, Visual Basic Scripting or VBS, and JScript. Shell scripting on the Windows platform is commonly used to produce logon scripts, which are in turn used to configure the Windows environment for specific uses when they log on. Marketing personnel for instance may use such scripts to automatically map network drives to the marketing network folder, and so on.

Despite what assembly code and C coders might tell us, high-level languages do have their place in every programmer's toolbox, and some of them are much more than a computer-science curiosity. Out of the many high-level languages we can choose from today, Python seems to be the most interesting for those who want to learn something new and do real work at the same time. Its no-nonsense implementation of object-oriented programming and its clean and easy-to-understand syntax make it a language that is fun to learn and use, which is not something we can say about most other languages.

In Python Training, you will learn how to write applications that use command-line options, read and write to pipes, access environment variables, handle interrupts, read from and write to files, create temporary files and write to system logs. In other words, you will find recipes for writing real applications instead of the old boring Hello, World! stuff.

Getting Started

To begin, if you have not installed the Python interpreter on your system, now is the time. To make that step easier, install the latest Python distribution using packages compatible with your Linux distribution. rpm, deb and tgz are also available on your Linux CD-ROM or on-line. If you follow standard installation procedures, you should not have any problems.

I also recommend that you have the Python Library Reference handy; you might want it when the explanations given here do not meet your needs. You can find it in the same places as the Python Tutorial.

Creating scripts can be done using your favorite text editor as long as it saves text in plain ASCII format and does not automatically insert line breaks when the line is longer than the width of the editor's window.

Always begin your scripts with either

#! /usr/local/bin/python

or

#! /usr/bin/python

If the access path to the python binary on your system is different, change that line, leaving the first two characters (#!) intact. Be sure this line is truly the first line in your script, not just the first non-blank line-it will save you a lot of frustration.

Use chmod to set the file permissions on your script to make it executable. If the script is for you alone, type chmod 0700 scriptfilename.py; if you want to share it with others in your group but not let them edit it, use 0750 as the chmod value; if you want to give access to everyone else, use the value 0755. For help with the chmod command, type man chmod.

Reading Command-Line Options and Arguments

Command-line options and arguments come in handy when we want to tell our scripts how to behave or pass some arguments (file names, directory names, user names, etc.) to them. All programs can read these options and arguments if they want, and your Python scripts are no different.

Bash script can be utilized for different purposes, for example, executing a shell order, running various directions together, tweaking managerial errands, performing task robotization and so on. So information of slam programming nuts and bolts is significant for each Linux client. This section will assist you with getting the fundamental thought on slam programming. A large portion of the regular activities of slam scripting are clarified with extremely basic models here.

Bash script can be utilized for different purposes, for example, executing a shell direction, running various directions together, modifying managerial errands, performing task robotization and so on. So learning of slam programming nuts and bolts is significant for each

Linux client. This part will assist you with getting the essential thought on slam programming.

A typical example of bash scripting is sh-bang #!/bin/bash -e and an example of python scripting is magic 8-ball and port scanner in phyth

Chapter 7 Wireless Hacking

The proliferation of readily available Wi-Fi networks has made Wi-Fi one of the most common network mediums. Wi-Fi is in many ways superior to traditional copper wire physically connected networks. Aside from the convenience of connectivity and the flexibility of network configurations that wireless networks afford the users, the lack of physical infrastructure needed to complete the network makes it much cheaper and easier to implement than Ethernet. With this convenience, however, comes certain security concerns that are not associated with traditional hardwired networks. With a copper or fiber-based network, a physical connection is needed for a new machine to join the network. A hacker would normally have difficulty accessing the physical space of a target network and would likely arouse suspicion attempting to connect their own hardware to network cabling. Although the range of Wi-Fi is limited, it is omnidirectional and the radiofrequency signals admitted by the server and the various nodes on a wireless network traverse walls and other barriers and can be intercepted by anyone in range. This gives the hacker much more freedom to conduct a network intrusion without being detected.

Hacking Wi-Fi

Most Wi-Fi networks consist of a wireless router, or a group of wireless routers, that are connected to a modem which is delivering internet access to some physical location. The routers broadcast and receive radio signals on specific channels that carry the appropriate TCP/IP packets to and from other machines and devices that have similar wireless connectivity. All nodes communicating at any given time on the channels associated with the router or routers that are connected to the modem at that location comprise a Wi-Fi network. By nature, Wi-Fi networks are very dynamic and fluid. Especially in commercial settings, like coffee shops or office buildings that provide wireless access, the number and nature of the nodes on that particular network are in constant flux. In these public settings, it is easy for a hacker to hide in plain sight and attempt to intrude into any of the nodes on the network. Once the hacker is successfully on the network itself, they can scan the network for all connected machines and probe for vulnerabilities. Many networks have both wireless and wired subnetworks that are interconnected. When a hacker gains access to a wireless network they can conceivably use that to leverage access to all of the nodes on the wired portion of the network. This makes Wi-Fi hacking a very popular goal for modern hackers.

Wi-Fi Encryption Protocols

Since Wi-Fi signals are broadcast into the air as opposed to being confined within wires, it is important for the information contained in the signals to be encrypted. Otherwise, anyone could passively receive and view any information being sent between the nodes on the network. The encryption protocols used in Wi-Fi have necessarily evolved since wireless networks began gaining popularity. Moreover, as technology has improved and resulted in increased bandwidth and data rates, a great density of information can be broadcast from a wireless network in a very short period of time, making it especially important for it to be encrypted and kept out of the hands of malicious hackers.

The oldest and most common Wi-Fi encryption protocol is Wired Equivalent Privacy (WEP). The goal of the WEP standard, as the name implies, was to give network users the same amount of security that they would have on a physically connected network. Unfortunately, over time WEP has become the least secure of all of the existing encryption protocols and it is quite easily hacked by even the most inexperienced hackers. WEP is so insecure in fact, that many Wi-Fi router manufacturers no longer provide that type of encryption as an option on their hardware. Most security professionals recommend that router owners do not use WEP when other options are available. Step-by-step instructions and coding examples for attacking WEP protected Wi-Fi networks are freely and readily available on the internet. Although the level of encryption has increased from 64 bit to 128 bit to 256 bit, the underlying flaws in WEP remain easily exploitable by even the most green of neophyte hackers. The biggest problem with WEP is that a password can be quickly and easily deciphered simply through the passive "sniffing" (receiving and viewing network packets) of network traffic.

A significant step up from WEP Wi-Fi encryption is the Wi-Fi Protected Access (WPA) standard of encryption. This new protocol fixed many of the problems in WEP, but remained vulnerable to attack because it was still based on some of the same underlying encryption algorithms. Furthermore, WPA-protected routers were deployed with a feature that was designed to make it more convenient for home users to connect new devices to their network. This feature proved to be an additional vulnerability in systems that employed WPA.

It wasn't long before an update to WPA was needed to keep Wi-Fi networks more secure. A new encryption standard being used in other secure applications, the Advanced Encryption Standard (AES), became mandatory in the new Wi-Fi encryption protocol which became known as WPA-2. WPA-2 with AES encryption has become the recommended setting for wireless routers on which it is available because of its significant improvement in security over its preceding standards. Cracking WPA and WPA-2 requires more intrusive hacking techniques than the simple passive sniffing that can be used to attack WEP-protected networks.

Wi-Fi Attacks

In order to conduct a Wi-Fi attack a hacker needs, at a minimum, a computer (normally a laptop) that can run scripts which are used to decipher the Wi-Fi password. They also must acquire a special Wi-Fi adapter that can be purchased relatively cheaply. A list of suitable Wi-Fi adapters can be found on hacker resource websites, but in general the adapter must have a feature known as "monitor mode" in order to be able to execute a Wi-Fi attack. It is important to note that not all Wi-Fi adapters that can be found at retail computer supply stores have this feature, and most internal laptop adapters are not appropriate. In general, hackers prefer to use some sort of Linux distribution, usually Kali, to conduct a Wi-Fi attack because most of the readily available tools were written for the Linux OS and come preinstalled on Kali. It is also possible with some configuration to run Linux on a virtual machine within another OS to mount a successful attack. Although attacks from other operating systems are possible, it is much easier for the beginner to conduct them from either a native Linux distribution or a virtual machine. A hacker-friendly distribution like Kali is recommended.

The detailed procedures and recommended programs for conducting Wi-Fi attacks against the various encryption protocols changes over time, although the general principles are the same. For the simplest attack, which is against WEP encryption, the general steps are as follows:

1) monitor and view all Wi-Fi traffic in the range of the adapter while in "monitor mode" (set by a program called *airmon-ng*) using a program called *airodump-ng.*

Live W-Fi Traffic on Several Routers (aircrack-ng.org)

2) choose a target Wi-Fi network that is using WEP encryption and make a note of the name (ESSID) and network address (BSSID in the form XX:XX:XX:XX:XX:XX)

3) restart *airodump-ng* to begin capturing network traffic from the specific network that you are targeting

4) wait for a sufficient number of packets to be captured (this may take longer on networks with less traffic)

5) use a program called *aircrack-ng* to piece together the captured network packets into a coherent password

A Successfully Decrypted Wi-Fi Key (aircrack-ng.org)

If network traffic is too slow to capture a sufficient number of packets for decrypting the password in a reasonable period of time, some hackers choose to use a program called *aireplay-ng* to inject artificial packets into the network and create the necessary traffic to crack it more quickly. However, this activity requires the hacker's machine to actually broadcast signals from its Wi-Fi adapter, making it more conspicuous.

WPA encryption cannot be cracked passively and requires the additional step of packet injection. Cracking WPA can

take longer and is a more invasive procedure, but it is not much more difficult than cracking WEP. A program called *reaver*, normally available on the Kali distribution is typically used by hackers to crack WPA. WPA-2 hacking is a much more advanced concept for more experienced practitioners. (Note: the software tools above are pre-installed on Kali Linux, or can be downloaded from www.aircrack-ng.org)

Chapter 8 Your First Hack

The neophyte hacker shouldn't even think about attempting an attack on a real target as their first foray into hacking. Sufficient tools and technologies exist which are easily obtained and with which various methods can be rehearsed in a virtual environment. This type of practice is essential for the hacker and is more valuable than all of the reading and study one could accomplish. To build confidence and gain appreciation for the nuances and practical pitfalls, the beginning hacker should aspire to accomplish the simple attacks suggested in this chapter. The details of the attacks will vary and currently applicable instructions should be researched by the reader, but the general principles of the setup and execution should be fairly universal.

Hacking Your Own Wi-Fi

The purpose of this practice attack is to successfully obtain the password of a WEP-encrypted Wi-Fi network. To minimize risk, the network and any connected devices should be owned or controlled by you, or by someone who has given you explicit permission to perform penetration testing.

What you need:

1) A computer
2) A wireless network adapter that supports "monitor mode"
3) Access to a Wi-Fi router with WEP encryption (does not have to have internet access)
4) The latest version of Kali Linux (installed as the primary OS or in a virtual machine)

Setting up:

1) Ensure that the router is set to WEP and give it a password of your choice
2) Turn off the internal Wi-Fi adapter on your laptop if you have one
3) Connect the "monitor mode" adapter to your attack machine and install any necessary drivers
4) Be sure the attack computer is in wireless range of the target network

Procedure:

1) Follow the "Wi-Fi Hacking" steps
2) Confirm that the cracked password matches the one you set for the network
3) Repeat the hack using aireplay-ng for packet injection and compare execution times

4) Change the length or complexity of the password and repeat the hack, comparing execution times

A Virtual Windows Vulnerability Assessment

Operating systems contain multiple software vulnerabilities that hackers are ready and willing to exploit. When a hacker discovers an un-patched version of an OS, there are a number of commonly available exploits with which to gain access. The first step in deploying those exploits is to analyze the OS for the most glaring vulnerabilities. Kali Linux features natively installed tools that will scan a system and provide a list of vulnerabilities. This exercise will require two virtual machines running within the same system (regardless of the host OS). It will also require an installation image for an older, unsupported, and un-patched version of Microsoft Windows (Windows '95 or '98 are good choices). These images can be obtained online (usgcb.nist.gov) or from an old CD.

What you need:

1) A computer with any OS
2) Virtualization software
3) The latest version of Kali Linux
4) An unsupported, un-patched version of Microsoft Windows

Setting up:

1) Install Kali Linux on a virtual machine
2) Install the target Windows distribution on a virtual machine (on the same host system as Kali)

Procedure:

1) Execute a network scan from the Kali virtual machine using a program called *nmap*
2) Practice changing various settings in *nmap* so that OS vulnerabilities will be detected and displayed
3) Make note of the listed Windows vulnerabilities and begin researching exploits!

Chapter 9 Scanning Ports

The reason you are going to want to scan ports is so that you can find an open one. With ports, you are going to be able to get into someone's system and leave a door open so that you can get in again later on. Port scans use host scans which can take up a lot of time if you have a wide range of IP addresses that have to be scanned and most of them end up being vacant.

Ports That Are Open

A network scanner is going to be used when you are connected to either of these ports and as soon as the port accepts the connection from the scanner, it is going to be best for you to assume that the program that is bound is running as it should be.

TCP ports are going to work with SYN packets that are sent back and forth between the servers, and the clients use them. Whenever the packet is sent to the server, it is going to send a SYN/ACK packet back resulting in the client sending the ACK packet back. After the SYN packet is received once more by the client, the port is going to be opened. In the off chance that an RST packet is sent instead, then the port is going to be closed. If the server does not send anything, then there is probably a firewall that is blocking it from the port or the port is not running on that IP address.

When you are scanning UDP ports, you are going to most likely run into problems because there are no handshakes exchanged and the programs are going to get rid of any packets that they are not going to be able to process. UDP packets are going to be sent to a port without a program that is bound to it. ICMP error packets are going to be what is returned. From there you are most likely going to consider the port to be closed. No answer is going to mean that a firewall is filtering out the packets or the port is opened. Too many people end up leaving their UDP scans because these scanners have difficulty telling the difference between when a port is opened and when it is filtering the packets.

Ports That Are More Common

To save yourself some time, Nmap is going to scan around 1667 ports that are going to be the default ports. But, you are going to get more results if you thoroughly scan all the ports; and there are 65536 ports. So, if you have the time, scan them all!

Port Specifications

When you are using the -p command, you are going to be able to tell the Nmap program exactly which ports you want it to scan so that you can save time on your scanning.

Target Specifications

Just like you can tell Nmap to scan specific ports, you can also tell it to go after a specific host or set of hosts. This host is going to be verified only by putting in the IP address for that host or by using the domain name. Should you wish to scan several different ports, you are going to want to set up the range for the IP addresses.

Scan Types

TCP SYN

A TCP SYN scan is going to be the default scan done by Nmap. When you use the -sS command, the program will only do that scan. As the administrator, you are going to be allowed to start the scan. If a user starts the scan, then a connect scan is going to be performed.

TCP connect

There is a command that you can use to make sure that Nmap has a full connection and that is the -sT command. This scan is not going to be as good as the TCP SYN scan because there is more that has to be sent back and forth between the client and the server. This scan is going to be executed with user privileges or whenever an IPv6 address is being scanned.

TCP null

When you use the -sN option, the program is going to send back all packets that do not have anything to do with SYN, ACK, or RST flags. If it comes back that the port is closed, the RST packet is going to be the one returned. If the port is opened or has a firewall filtering its packets, then there is not going to be a response sent back. Doing a null scan is going to be the best way to attempt to get passed the stateless firewall however if the firewall is stateful then it is not going to do anything.

UDP empty packet

When you use the -sU function, Nmap is going to send out UDP packets that contain no data. If an error message is returned, then you are going to assume that the port is closed. However, when there is no response, you will assume the port is opened or filtered. This scan cannot tell the difference between a filtered port or an open port which is going to leave some severe limitation in your scan.

UDP application

You are going to use -SU or -SV options to tell the program that you want data from an application or for the application to be identified. Since this has several different options put together, you are going to experience a slow scan.

Scanning Speed

Like most things, if things are sent at a speed that is faster than the system can deal with, then the packets are going to be dropped, and they are not going to be used in the scan thus you are going to get results that are not accurate. If there is an intrusion detection or an intrusion prevention that is in place on the target's network, then the faster that the scan is going through, the more likely that it is that you are going to be detected by the target.

There are a lot of devices as well as firewalls that work with IPS that are meant to respond to SYN packets that are sent in from the cookies created by these packets so that every port appears open even if they are not. When you are running a scan at full speed, then you are going to risk wreaking havoc on the network devices that are stateful.

With Nmap, there will be five templates that you can use to adjust the speed in case it does not adjust itself properly. With the -T0 option, you are going to force the program to wait about five minutes in between sending packets. -T1 waits for fifteen seconds, -T2 for 0.4 seconds, and -T3 which is going to be the default setting where the timing goes unchanged. Lastly, when -T4 is used, the timeouts are reduced, but the retransmission speed is upped ever so slightly. -T5 is similar to -T4but things are going to be sped up even more. A modern IPS or IDS device is going to figure out the scans that are using -T1 and detect that device so that the hacker is discovered. As the user of Nmap, you can also decide to make a new template with new parameters if you are not happy with the ones that are provided.

Identifying Applications

If you decide to use the -SV option, then Nmap is going to have to figure out which version of the application is currently being run.

Identifying the Operating System

If you want to discover which operating system is being used by the target, you will use the -O option in Nmap. There are packets that are specially crafted to be sent to the target to all of the ports so that the responses can be analyzed in the database that you are using on your operating system.

Save

When you want to save the output that you get returned to you, you will use the -oX<filename> option so that it is saved in an XML format.

Chapter 10 Attacking With Frameworks

Social Engineering

Due to the increase in the use of technology for almost all of our activities, companies and organizations have invested a huge amount of money in ensuring that the technologies they use are properly secured from hackers. These companies have developed and implemented extensive firewalls to protect against any possible security breach. Most internet users are not security conscious despite the ease with which information can be obtained over an internet connection. This is coupled with the fact that most malicious hackers concentrate their efforts on computer servers and client application flaws. Over the years, these hackers have become more creative in how they gather information and structure their attacks on websites and web apps. With the enormous amount of money invested in online security, we would expect that malicious information theft or control would have been eliminated. However, this has not happened.

This is where we use social engineering to achieve our goal. It is a non-technical approach circumvents a company's security measures. No matter how secure a company's online applications are, they are still susceptible to hacking. Hackers have been able to achieve this using social engineering and tools based on social engineering. Social engineering is a hands-on approach to hacking. It involves targeting individuals and manipulating them into giving out vital information that can lead to a breach in the security system. These individuals, who may be employees of the organization or even a close relative of the top person at the target organization, are approached and coerced into trusting the hacker. They begin to gather information that could be of use in the hacking process. This is usually an approach taken when the company's firewalls are effective at thwarting outside penetration. When the hackers have obtained the necessary information (for instance, the login information of the social engineering target), they can hack the company from the inside out.

It is believed that human beings are the weakest link in any information security chain. The physical approach toward social engineering can occur in so many ways that it is impossible to cover all of them in this chapter. However, popular means include approaching and becoming friends with (or even a significant other of) employees at the company. Sometimes the employees are given a flash drive containing movies or other files in which they may be interested. The employees plug in the drive and launch a file that executes scripts in the background, granting the hackers access to the respective machines. The social engineer attack can also occur when a person calls an employee of a firm, impersonates a call center representative and tells the employee that he or she needs information to rectify a service that is important. The hacker would have gathered details about the employee from the employee's social media account or through personal conversations with the person. Once the hacker has received the information (which may include the victim's social security number or login details), the hacker hijacks the account and performs fraudulent transactions on it, or uses it for additional attacks. Social engineering makes it easy to build a username and password list that helps with logging into the target's accounts.

Hackers use the information they have gathered in combination with tools that ensure an easy hack of the company's system. Most of these tools are used in the client-side attack and are enhanced with the information gathered through social engineering. This information is used in conjunction with phishing and spoofing tools to attack a client if a direct social engineering attack fails. Social engineering is the information gathering procedure in this approach when it comes to attacking clients. Hacking has become a business venture. Hackers gain access to information simply to sell it for money, or to use it to transfer money. The motivation now is monetary. Usually, the target is selected, and the hacker uses information available to the public about the client to develop the attack. Typically, information obtained online is sufficient to build an attack. However, with an increase in employee education regarding hackers and social engineering, employees have begun to limit the personal information they share on social media and other public platforms.

The success of a social-engineering-based attack depends solely on the quality of information gathered. The attacker must be sociable and persuasive when interacting with the victim, such that the victim becomes open and begins to trust the hacker. Some hackers outsource this aspect to an individual who is skilled in getting people to tell them secrets.

Social Engineering Toolkit (SET)

The Social Engineering Toolkit is a very important tool used in a computer-aided social engineering attack. It comes pre-installed with the Kali Linux distro. It is written in the Python language and is also an open source toolkit. The Social Engineering Toolkit, or SET, was created by David Kennedy to exploit the human aspect of web security. However, it is important to make sure that the Social Engineering Toolkit is up to date. Once the tool has been updated, the configuration file can be set. The default configuration file is sufficient to make the SET run without any problems. Advanced users may want to edit and tweak certain settings. However, if you are a beginner, it is better to leave it the way it is until you become more familiar with the Social Engineering Toolkit. To access the configuration file, open the terminal and then change the directory to the SET. Open the config folder and you will find the set_config file, which you can open and edit with a text editor to change the parameters.

The Social Engineering Toolkit can be accessed by clicking on the Application icon, then clicking on the Kali Linux desktop. Next, click on BackTrack and then on the Exploitation Tools option. Click on Social Engineering

Tools and select the Social Engineering Toolkit by clicking on SET. The SET will open in a terminal window. Alternatively, the SET can be opened directly from the terminal by typing "setoolkit" without the quotes.

The Social Engineering Toolkit opens in the terminal as a menu-based option. The menu contains different options based on the type of social engineering attack you need to use. The option at number 1 is for spear-phishing vectors which enable the user to execute a phishing attack. The phishing attack is an email attack. It is like casting a net by sending emails to random potential victims. Spear-phishing, on the other hand, targets one individual and the email is more personalized.

The second option on the SET menu is the website attack vector, which uses different web-attack methods against its target victim. The website attack vector option is by far the most popular and perhaps most used option in the Social Engineering Toolkit. Clicking on the website attack vector option opens menus containing the Java applet attack vector, the Metasploit browser exploits, the credential harvester attack used in cloning websites, the tabnabbing attack, the man-in-the-middle attack, the web jacking attack and the multi-attack web method.

The third option on the Social Engineering Toolkit menu is the infectious media generator tool. This is a very easy tool to use and is targeted at individuals who can give a hacker access to the organization network, thus enabling the hacker to hack from inside the network. This tool allows the hacker to create a USB disk or DVD containing a malicious script that gives the hacker access to the target shell. Choosing this option opens a menu with a prompt to choose from between a file-format exploit or a standard Metasploit executable. Choosing the file-format option opens a list of payloads from which to select. The default is a PDF file embedded in an executable script. This is then sent to the drive where the autorun.inf is created with the PDF file. When an employee opens the file on the drive, the file is executed in the background and the hacker gains shell access to the victim's computer.

The fourth option is the generate-a-payload-with-listener option. This option allows the hacker to create a malicious script as a payload and therefore generate a listener. This script is a .exe file. The key is getting the intended victim to click and download this script. Once the victim downloads the .exe file and executes it, the listener alerts the hacker, who can access the victim's shell.

The fifth option in the Social Engineering Toolkit is the mass mailer option. Clicking this option brings up a menu with two options: single email address attack and the mass mailer email attack. The single email address attack allows the user to send an email to a single email address while the mass mailer email attack allows the user to send an email to multiple email addresses. Choosing this option prompts the user to select a list containing multiple email addresses to which the email is then sent.

Sixth on the list is the Arduino-based attack. With this option, you are given the means to compromise Arduino-based devices. The seventh option, on the other hand, is the SMS spoofing option, which enables the hacker to send SMS to a person. This SMS spoofing option opens a menu with an option to perform an SMS spoofing form of attack or create a social-engineering template. Selecting the first option will send to a single number or a mass SMS attack. Selecting just a single number prompts the user to enter the recipient's phone number. Then you are asked to either use a predefined template or craft your own message. Typing 1 chooses the first option while typing 2 chooses the second option depending on your preference for the SMS. Then you enter the source number, which is the number you want the recipient to see as the sender of the SMS. Next, you type the message you want the recipient to see. You can embed links to a phishing site or to a page that will cause the user to download a malicious .exe file. After the message has been crafted, the options for services used in SMS spoofing appear on the screen. Some are paid options and others are free.

Option eight in the SET is the wireless AP attack vector. This option is used to create a fake wireless AP to which unsuspecting users of public Wi-Fi can connect and the hacker can sniff their traffic. This option uses other applications in achieving this goal. AirBase-NG, AirMon-NG, DNSSpoof and dhcpd3 are the required applications that work hand in hand with the wireless AP attack vector.

Option nine in the menu is the QR code attack vector. Today, QR codes are used everywhere, from the identification of items to obtaining more details about products on sale. Now QR codes are even used to make payments. Some websites use QR codes for logins or as web apps. This login method is used because it is perceived as a more secure way of gaining access due to hackers' being able to steal cookies, execute a man-in-the-middle attack and even use a brute-force password to gain unauthorized access. However, this increase in the use of QR codes has given hackers more avenues for exploiting their victims. The QR code attack vector helps the hacker create a malicious QR code. Then the hacker creates or clones a website like Facebook using the credential harvester option and embeds this malicious QR code with the link to the cloned website. The hacker then sends a phishing email or spoofed SMS to a victim, which prompts that person to scan the code with a mobile device. This reveal's the victim's GPS location and other information when the victim visits the website and enters their login details.

The tenth option in the menu is the PowerShell attack vector. This option allows the hacker to deploy payloads in the PowerShell of an operating system. The PowerShell is a more powerful option than the command prompt in the Windows operating system. It allows access to different areas of the operating system. It was developed by Microsoft to ease the automation of tasks and configuration of files and has come with the Windows operating system since the release of Windows Vista. The PowerShell attack vector enables the attacker to create a script that is then executed in the victim's PowerShell. The selection of this option brings out four menu options: PowerShell alphanumeric injector,

PowerShell SAM database, PowerShell reverse and PowerShell bind shells. Any of these options creates a targeted PowerShell program and is exported to the PowerShell folder. Tricking the target to access, download and execute this program creates access for the attacker.

By now, you should realize how powerful the SET is in executing computer-aided social engineering attacks. This tool is very valuable for a penetration tester, as it provides a robust and diverse means of checking the various vulnerabilities that may exist in an organization's network.

BeEF

BeEF stands for Browser Exploitation Framework. This tool comes with most of the security-based Linux distro, like the Parrot OS and Kali Linux. BeEF started as a server that was accessed through the attacker's browser. It was created to target vulnerabilities in web browsers that would give access to the target systems for executing commands. BeEF was written in the Ruby language on the Rails platform by a team headed by Wade Alcorn. As stated before, passwords, cookies, login credentials and browsing history are all typically stored on the browser, so a BeEF attack on a client can be very nasty.

On Kali Linux, however, BeEF has been included in the distro. The BeEF framework can be started by going into applications, clicking on exploitation tools and then clicking on the BeEF XSS framework. This brings up a terminal that shows the BeEF framework server has been started. Once the server has been started, we open our browser of choice and visit the localhost at port 3000. This is written in the URL space of the browser as localhost:3000/ui/authentication or 127.0.0.1:3000/ui/authentication. This would bring us to the authentication page of the BeEF framework, requiring a login username and password. By default, the username is beef ; the password is also beef.

Once you are in the BeEF framework, it will open a "Get Started" tab. Here you are introduced to the framework and learn how to use it. Of particular importance is hooking a browser. Hooking a browser involves clicking a JavaScript payload that gives the BeEF framework access to the client's browser. There are various ways by which we can deploy this payload, but the simplest way is to create a page with the payload, prompt the target to visit that page and execute the JavaScript payload. You can be very creative about this aspect. On the other hand, there is a link on the Get Started page that redirects you to The Butcher page. Below this page are buttons containing the JavaScript payload. Clicking on this button will execute the script and, in turn, hook your browser. When your browser is hooked, you will see a hook icon beside your browser icon on the left side of the BeEF control panel with the title "Hooked browser" along with folders for online and offline browsers.

Once a browser is hooked, whether it's online or offline, we can control it from our BeEF control panel. Clicking on the details menu in the control panel will provide information like the victim's browser version and the plugins that are installed. The window size of the browser also can be used to determine the victim's screen size, the browser platform (which is also the operating system on the PC), and a lot more information. For executing commands on the browser, we click on the command menu in the control panel. This brings up a different command we can execute on the victim's browser. This command would create a pop-up message on the victim's browser, so it can be renamed creatively before execution to avoid raising any suspicion. Some of the commands that can be executed in this menu include the Get all Cookie command (which starts harvesting the victim's browser cookies), the Screenshot command, the Webcam command for taking pictures of the victim, the Get visited URL command and so on. There are a lot of commands in this menu.

The BeEF framework JavaScript payload can also hook mobile phone browsers. Checking the details tab after hooking will give that particular information if we end up hooking a phone browser. Clicking on the module and searching the PhoneGap command allows us to execute phone targeted commands like geolocating the device and starting an audio recording on the victim's device. Clicking on the Ipec menu also displays a terminal we can use to send shell commands to the victim's system.

Once the BeEF framework hooks a browser, the possibilities are endless. We can do virtually anything. Therefore, it is important to be careful when clicking links and pop-up or flash messages.

METASPLOIT

The Metasploit framework is perhaps the larget, most complete penetration testing and security auditing tool today. This tool is an open source tool that is regularly updated with new modules for monitoring even the most recent vulnerabilities. Metasploit comes with the Kali Linux distro. It is written in Ruby, although when it was created it was written in Perl. This tool was developed by HD Moore in 2003 and was then sold to an IT company called Rapid7 in 2009.

Metasploit is an immensely powerful tool that has great versatility. To fully utilize Metasploit, you must be comfortable using the terminal, which is a console type window. However, there is an option that allows for the use of Metasploit in a GUI window. Armitage, an opensource tool, makes this possible, although it does not have the capacity to fully utilize all aspects of the Metasploit framework in an attack. The meterpreter in the Metasploit framework is a module that is dumped in the victim's system, making it easy for the hacker to control that PC and maintain access for future hacks in that system. Getting started with Metasploit on Kali Linux is as good as opening the terminal and typing "msfconsole" without the quotes.

Metasploit contains modules that can be used during a hack. Some of these modules are written by developers or contributors from the open source community. An important set of modules includes the payloads. The payloads are very important when it comes to performing attacks within the Metasploit framework. These payloads are codes that have been written so that the hacker can gain a foothold in the victim's computer. Perhaps the most popular among these payloads is the meterpreter. This particular payload is very powerful, as it leaves no trace of a hack on the system's drive. It exists solely on the victim's system memory.

Then there is the Exploits module. These exploits are codes that have been written and packed for specific flaws in a victim's operating system. Different exploits exist for different operating system flaws, so flaws that are targeted for one vulnerability would fail when used for another.

The encoders are modules that encode the different payloads deployed into the target system to avoid detection by the victim's antivirus, anti-spyware or other security tools.

Other modules available on the Metasploit framework are the Post modules (which allow the hacker to gather passwords, tokens and hashes), the Nops modules (most of which allow for 100 percent execution of the payload or exploit) and the Auxiliary modules (which do not fit into other categories).

This framework is quite robust, as many kinds of hacking procedures can be carried out. Several procedures are executed by combining the modules and making them work in different ways. A good way for a beginner to learn more about the Metasploit framework is to type "help" without the quotes in the Metasploit framework console.

Chapter 11 Strategies To Combat Cyber Terrorist Threats

Implement strategic plans to counter cyber terrorist efforts will ensure that your organization has the means to combat any threats it may face. There are a number of strategies which a business can employee or in order to stay ahead and heighten their security capabilities in the face of a threat. These are:

Prosecuting Perpetrators

Many attacks can behind the wall of anonymity with many smaller organizations failing to pursue and prosecute the hackers responsible. While this can be a costly activity, there are some advantages in identifying and taking the attackers to court. This can be a shock to the cyber terrorist community and set the standard for which other organizations should conduct themselves in the wake of an attack. If the case is particularly high profile, the organization can benefit from the hard-line response with the prosecuted hackers being an example to the rest of the criminal organizations that are determined to wreak havoc on your business. This example set can send waves throughout the rest of the community and can lead to improvements in the investigation and prosecution process of criminal cyber terrorists. Therefore, is always in the best interest of the parties that have been affected by an attack to seek justice.

Develop New Security Practices

Take a Proactive Approach

It is important for both corporations and the general public to take a proactive approach as the threat from cyber terrorism becomes more sophisticated and targeted. This involves keeping up to date with the latest information within the cyber security sphere such as threats, vulnerabilities and noteworthy incidents as they will allow security professionals to gain a deeper insight into how these components could affect their organizations. From there they are able to develop and implement stronger security measures thereby reducing the opportunities for hackers to exploit for cyber-attacks.

Organizations should constantly be on the forefront of cyber security having a multi-level security infrastructure in order to protect valuable data and user's private information. All activities that are critical in nature should have security audits frequently to ensure all policies and procedures relating to security are adhered to. Security should be treated as an ongoing and continuous process rather than an aftermath of the consequences of an attack.

Deploy Vital Security Applications

There are many tools available for security professionals to protect their networks and they can provide a significant benefit to the job at hand. These applications involve firewalls, IDS, as well as anti-virus software that can ensure better protections against potential hackers. Using these security systems, security personnel are able to record, monitor and report any suspicious activities that can indicate the system is at risk. The applications are able to streamline the process, making the job far more efficient and effective. Utilizing these types of tools ensures that security personnel are assisted with the latest in prevention technology and have a greater probability of combating attackers.

Establish Business Disaster Recovery Plans

In the event that an attack does occur, all businesses should have a worst-case scenario contingency plan in place to ensure that processes and operations are brought back to normally as soon as possible. Without such plans, the consequences can be disastrous leading to a loss in revenue and reputation on behalf of the business. Once these plans have been devised, they should be rehearsed regularly in order to test their effectiveness and also provide staff with training in the event of an attack.

These plans should be comprised of two main components, these being, repair and restoration. From the perspective of repair, the attacking force should be neutralised as soon as possible with the objective to return operations to normalcy and have all functions up and running. The restoration element is geared towards having pre-specified arrangements with hardware, software as well as a network comprised of service vendors, emergency services and public utilities on hand to assist in the restoration process.

Cooperation with Other Firms

Your organization would not be alone in dealing with the aftermath of a cyber-attack. Many organizations exist in order to deal with cyber terrorism threats both public and private. These groups can go a long way in helping with issues relating to cyber terrorism such as improving the security within your organization, helping devise and implement disaster recovery plans and further discuss how you can deal with threats in the future and what this means for the wider community. Having this extended network available to you will enhance your efforts in resisting cyber-attacks as well as having a role in discussing other emerging threats and protecting organizations facing these same threats.

Increasing Security Awareness

It is important not to become complacent in times where security threats are prevalent and this requires an increase in awareness with all issues relating to cyber security. Having your organization become an authority in raising awareness within the community will help educate other organizations in how they can defend themselves against attacks and strengthen their own security which in turn will damage the cyberterrorist community as they face a stronger resistance. You can also raise awareness within your own organization through security training programs which will help all employees equip themselves with the right skillset to combat threats that could arise through their own negligence and will also help them be more alert in times when threats could be present.

Chapter 12 Tails

Edward Snowden. The name rings a bell for most people around the globe. In tech circles he is a visionary. As for the non-techies, a few labels come to mind: Whistleblower. Hero. Traitor. Regardless of what you pin him with, one thing is certain: He hates censorship and loves anonymity, the kind of anonymity that calls for untrackable execution. Before discussing anything, he insisted liaisons use not only *PGP* (pretty good privacy) but the end-all-be-all of anonymity tools: *Tails*-- a thief-simple tool that frustrates even those in the upper echelon of the NSA. And for good reason, since even they do not know the wizard who designed it.

Where Tor is the worm of the anonymous fisherman, Tails is the fishing box. The fish at the other end have no idea who is inside the boat, watching, listening. It's a hacker's tool but also a patriot weapon. Using it is a breeze: install it on a USB stick, CD, whatever, boot from said stick and find yourself cloaked and shielded from the NSA, provided that you don't out yourself. And if you're using Tails, you're smarter than that anyway.

Built upon the shell of Linux, it acts as an operating system and comes with an assortment of nukes to launch under Big Brother's nose: Tor browser, chat client, email, office suite and image/sound editor, among others.

Snowden preferred Tails on account of its no-write rule: no direct data writing. A breach from a remote adversary? Not going to happen. Forensics investigation? Nope. No trace is going to be left on the DVD/USB. Obviously this is a no brainer to use if you're an NSA employee looking to spill the beans on unconstitutional spying, as well as a must-have for political dissidents and journalists. It is armored with plausible deniability, the same as Truecrypt.

Tor runs like warm butter when you boot with Tails. There's not much of a learning curve, and no excessive tweaking required. You can use it in the same PC you use at work. Boot from USB or DVD. Do your thing then reboot back into your normal PC with no record or footprint of your Tailing. For all intents, you're a ghost on the internet. And speaking of ghosts, the creators of Tails are anonymous themselves. No one knows their identities. But what we do know is that they will not bow to governments trying to muscle a backdoor into the code.

Linus Torvalds, creator of Linux, said in 2013, "The NSA has been pressuring free software projects and developers in various ways," implying that they had made the effort, and all with taxpayer funds. A bit like the cat saying to the mouse, "Transparency is good for you. Sleep out in the open and not the damp and dark, flea-infested mousehole." They don't like secrets.

You might be asking, how do we *know* that Tails does not already *have* a backdoor? How do we know that the NSA has not already greased their hands? The evidence is twofold: the code is open-source (anyone can audit it), and the mere fact that the NSA made an effort to sideline end-users says they fear such a powerful package. They cannot peer inside to see what the mice are doing. Snowden claimed that the NSA, while he was with them, was a major thorn in the side of that organization.

At the time of Tails conception five years ago, the interest had already started to build up in the Tor community for a more cohesive toolbox. "At that time some of us were already Tor enthusiasts and had been involved in free software communities for years," they said. "But we felt that something was missing to the panorama: a toolbox that would bring all the essential privacy enhancing technologies together and made them ready to use and accessible to a larger public."

PGP is also included in package. You owe it to yourself and peace of mind to learn it. Spend a Sunday with it and you'll be a competent user. Spend a week and you'll be an enthusiast. As well, *KeePassX* can be useful if you want to store different info (usernames, pass phrases, sites, comments) into one database. These two are like a good set of gauntlets no aspiring black knight would do without. And don't think the blacksmiths have just smelted down some cheap metal, either. The designers have gone to a lot of trouble to modify the privacy and security settings. The more they do, the less you have to.

But the true Achilles heel is the *metadata*. Tails is really lousy at hiding it. It doesn't try to. It doesn't clear any of it nor does it encrypt the headers of your encrypted emails. Are you an ebook author? Be careful about PDFs and .mobi files, as depending on which software you use, it can store the author's name and creation date of your work. But this is not really the fault of Tails. Rather, it is the wishes of the development team to stay compatible with the SMTP protocol.

The other problem with metadata is pictures: JPEGs, TIFF, BITMAPS and so on, which again, depending on the software, can store EXIF data--data that stores the date the picture was taken as well as the GPS coordinates of the image. Newer cameras and mobile phones like Samsung Galaxy are notorious for this, and even keep a thumbnail of the EXIF data intact for nose parkers with nothing to do all day but to sniff through other people's property. A *fake GPS spoofer* may be useful but even that won't eliminate the exif data. You'll need a separate *app* for this. You might even go so far as to only use formats that don't store any metadata at all. Plain-text is one option, though even that can be watermarked.

You might think, "Can I hide Tails activity?" The short answer is: maybe. It depends on the resources of the adversary. And just who is the adversary? The government? The private detective? The employer? The fingerprint Tails leaves is far less visible than what Tor leaves. And yes, it is possible for an administrator to see you are using Tor, as well as your ISP. They cannot tell what you're doing on Tor, mind you, but there are Tor Browser Bundle users, and Tails users. It all comes down to the sites you visit.

We've seen how they can build a profile on you from your resolution, window metrics, addons and extensions and time zones and fonts, but to alleviate this the Tails developers have tried to make everyone look the same, as if they were all wearing white Stormtrooper armor. Some fall through the cracks, making themselves easier for a correlation attack by installing too many addons and thus marking themselves in the herd: A purple-colored stormtrooper, if you will. Such and such user has a nice font enhancer while no other user does. This alone does not break anonymity, but with a hundred other factors and sufficient resources, it might be the one detail that breaks the house of cards. Death by a thousand stings.

You might find Tor *bridges* (alternative entry points on Tor) to be a good investment in reading, as they can better hide you from your ISP. In fact, using a bridge makes it considerably harder for your ISP to even know you are using Tor. If you decide this route (and you should if merely using Tor can get you arrested-- a case in which you should NOT use the default Tor configuration), the bridge address must be known.

Be mindful of the fact that a few bridges can be obtained on the Tor website. If you know about it, others do too-

-even adversaries like the NSA, but it is still stronger for anonymity purposes than the default Tor config. Like Freenet, it would be optimal if you personally know someone in a country outside the USA who runs a private obfuscated bridge that has the option *PublishServerDescriptor 0*. As always, luck favors the prepared.

Chapter 13 The Final Report

It is time now to send the client a final report with your feedback on all accomplished tasks.

It is important to stress how fundamental this part is. We need to present in a clear and complete manner all the information we gathered as well as each suggestion that could help to correct the weaknesses we spotted.

In addition to the list of vulnerabilities found and exploits used, we should include a part related to the so-called "remediation".

This part is meant to show the customer all the possible remedies for the risks we discovered.

It would be better to start the report with a general overview of the actions taken and then gradually enter into detail.

In this way, the report becomes easier to read for members of the management board and non-technicians, who will be able to understand exactly what is been reported.

Although we can also include other parts, a well-structured report usually consists of the following sections:

- Executive summary.
- Methodology used.
- Detailed analysis of the results.

Executive Summary

The executive summary is the report that can be understood even by non-technical staff, for example by managers.

First of all, we should define the scope and the estimated duration of this task.

By defining the scope of this task, we want to know exactly what type of penetration test we should perform and even more importantly what are the IP addresses or websites that we should include.

We must point out the evidences found and their level of criticality. We also need to prepare a graph showing the risk distribution according to the different variables:

Methodology

The methodology used integrates all the phases from the definition of the test scope to the final report.

We can summarize the procedure as follows:

- Definition of the test scope.
- Information gathering.
- Network scanning.
- Vulnerability assessment.
- Exploitation.
- Post exploitation.
- Other optional tests.
- Drafting of the report also through the use of automatic tools, for example with Dradis. (https://dradisframework.com/ce/).

As a side note, the report must also contain all the results you achieved that were related to the Web, including the **SQL Injection and XSS Cross Site Scripting**, which were not explained in this book.

You might also want to include the social engineering techniques you eventually used.

Detailed Analysis of The Results

The first task to complete in this sub-phase is defining the risk level of the various vulnerabilities you detected:

Then you can enlist all the vulnerabilities:

You can then conclude your report by mentioning the solutions and the suggestions that could help to block these risks and eradicate these problems.

Chapter 14 Banner Grabbing

This information will be useful to us in the next phase where we will look for vulnerabilities. In particular, the outdated version of a service could be exploited by a potential hacker.

We will start from the services normally associated with standard ports, and then move on the ones linked to unconventional ports.

Also, in this case we rely on a wizard that will lead us to define a specific service, make it active and try to grab the banner.

Installing The Web Server Microsoft Iis

We proceed with the installation of the IIS Web server directly from a **Windows Server 2012**.

You can refer to the following link for the installation steps: https://docs.microsoft.com/en-us/iis/get-started/whats- new-in-iis-8/8-installing-iis-on-windows-server-2012

At the end of the installation process, you can open your browser and type: *"http://127.0.0.1"*. If everything went well, this is what should appear on your screen:

We can see that IIS is listening by executing the "netstat" command and listening on port 80.

With the and filtering by port 80, we can see how the latter is listening:

Banner Visualization In Microsoft Iis

At this point, we must be able to grab the banner of our web server so that we can detect its type and version.

First of all, let's connect to the Web server using "*telnet*":

Once the channel has been set up, we can enter two commands that allow us to interact with the web server:

- GET / HTTP/1.1
- HOST: 127.0.0.1

This is what will appear on your screen:

We have captured the banner of our IIS web server. We can now identify the type of service and its version. This information will be useful during the vulnerability assessment phase.

Banner Configuration On Kfsensor

We should now use KFSensor to simulate a Microsoft IIS type web server.

Once the configuration is complete, we can use the Nmap feature called "**service detection**", which will attempt to grab the banner of the listening service and inform us of what version it is.

Nmap has correctly grabbed the banner and detected the exact version of the simulated service.

Installing A Ftp Server

We have previously installed a Microsoft web server. Now, instead, we will have to install an FTP server. You can find the installation steps at the following link: https://social.technet.microsoft.com/wiki/contents/artic les/12364.windows-server-2012-ftp-installation.aspx

Once the installation is complete, we can proceed with the creation of a new **FTP** site:

We are now listening port 21 without using SSL:

Ftp Banner Grabbing With Nmap

We can now capture the *FTP banner* using the Nmap service detection feature:

As you can see from the screenshot above, we have correctly detected the version of the FTP service running on the target machine.

Note that some system administrators may decide to obfuscate the banner for a certain service. We can also do this on the FTP server defined above:

Now we will no longer be able to detect the version of the service with Nmap:

Nmap was able to understand that port 21 is open. However, it does not provide any information about the version of the service running.

Ftp Banner Grabbing Wirh Metasploit

It is a tool that is used in the exploitation phase of a system. However, there are a number of additional modules that allow you to perform other activities, such as banner grabbing.

We start Metasploit by launching the "*msf*" command from terminal. Then we type the following command:

In "*rhost*", we need to enter the IP address of the victim machine, that is where the listening FTP service is located.

Once this part is completed, we can run the "**exploit**" command and then start the scanner:

The scan is quickly completed, and the result obtained informs us of the presence of a *Microsoft FTP server*. We grabbed the banner once again.

Ftp Banner Grabbing With Netcat

NETCAT is another useful tool used for grabbing banners. You can click here to learn more: https://en.wikipedia.org/wiki/Netcat.

Below is the command used to grab the banner:

Ftp Banner Grabbing With Telnet

We have already seen how the Telnet command works. Let's use it now to grab a banner:

Even in this case, we are able to correctly detect and grab the banner.

Operating System Detection

In addition to detecting a certain running service, it is also important to know the operating system present on a given machine.

We can follow two different procedures:

- Active mode.
- Passive mode.

In the active mode, we interact directly with the target. Nmap is a tool commonly used in active mode.

On the other hand, the passive mode listens to network traffic. Based on the characteristics of each operating system, we can obtain fairly precise information. A tool that works in this mode is **"P0f"** (https://it.wikipedia.org/wiki/P0f).

Os Detection With Nmap

Let's see how to detect the operating system of a certain machine using Nmap. The option to use is "-o", so this command will be the command we need to execute:

By running this command, we will examine only the first 100 doors and try to detect the operating system.

The result is the following:

Nmap was able to identify that the operating system in use is probably Windows and specifically version 7, 2012 or 8.1.

For more details, you might have to use other tools as well.

Os Detection With Xprobe

XPROBE is another tool useful for detecting the operating system. This is the command we should execute:

We should see the following results:

We are dealing with a Linux operating system, probably with 2.6.11 kernel.

Os Detection With P0f

As anticipated, this tool allows to perform a passive operating system detection. In this case, we do not need to interact directly with the target machine.

We need to capture some network traffic, so that **P0f** can complete the detection process. This is the command we should execute:

We press "*send*" and place the tool on hold:

We generate random traffic using, for example, the netcat:

This is the screen we will see if the traffic generated is enough for P0f:

As you can see, P0f informs us of what operating system version is currently used on the machine.

Chapter 15 Enumeration

Enumeration is an important phase of the penetration test process. It consists in exploiting the characteristics of a certain service in order to obtain as much information as possible.

There are services that work well with this type of investigation, such as

- SMTP, TCP port 25.
- DNS, UDP port 53.
- SNMP, UDP port 161.
- NETBIOS, UDP port 137,138; TCP port 139.

In this chapter, we will examine enumeration related to the following services:

- NETBIOS enumeration.
- DNS enumeration.
- Enumeration through DEFAULT PASSWORD.

Enumeration With Netbios

Netbios is a protocol that operates at the session layer of the **ISO/OSI model**. This protocol allows us to explore the network resources of computers, printers or files.

We can use Netbios to extract several information, including the following:

- *Hostname.*
- *Username.*
- *Domain.*
- *Printers.*
- Available network folders.

First of all, we should use Nmap to confirm that the TCP ports 139 and 445 are actually open:

nmap -v -p 139,445 192.169.1.120

After completing this step, we can use a special command, the **NBTSCAN**, to investigate systems with **open ports 139,445.**

We have a whole range of extracted **NETBIOS** information.

We can refer to another Windows command - "net view" - to continue our investigation on a specific host:

net view 192.168.1.10

It gives us the list of shared resources on our target. The "*net use*" command allows us to access these resources.

Nmap contains many scripts that can be used to enumerate <u>NETBIOS</u>. You can find them on the following path: /usr/share/nmap/scripts.

These are the scripts we need to verify any NETBIOS vulnerabilities:

- *smb-vuln-conficker.*
- *smb-vuln-cve2009-3103.*
- *smb-vuln-ms06-025.*
- *smb-vuln-ms07-029.*
- *smb-vuln-regsvc-dos.*
- *smb-vuln-ms08-067.*

Enumeration With Dns

With a single command we can extract different DNS records, which are the following ones:

- *SOA.*
- *A.*
- *MX.*
- *NS.*
- *CNAME.*
- *PTR.*
- *HINFO.*
- *TXT.*

We need to run this command:

<u>dnsenum domain.com</u>

Enumeration With Default Password

Network devices – such as routers and switches – very often have a default password. These passwords are defined directly by the device manufacturer. I would obviously suggest you change them as soon as possible.

DefaultPassword is one of the many sites where default device passwords are stored (https://default-password.info/).

This website is very easy to use. You just need to select the device model and manufacturer:

Chapter 16 Vulnerability Assessment

Thanks to network scanning, banner grabbing, and enumeration, we should have at this point a pretty good understanding of the types of services running on our network.

Now it's time to look for any vulnerabilities and we will use specific tools to carry out this activity.

A part of this research should be carried out manually, while we can use some tools to automate other parts of this process.

At this link, you can find a detailed report written by **SANS** that lists all the steps we should take to perform a *vulnerability* *Assessment:* https://www.sans.org/reading-room/whitepapers/basics/vulnerability-assessment-421.

I also want to clarify that, unlike vulnerability assessment, a penetration test has the additional purpose of exploiting the vulnerabilities found.

Below is the list of tools we will use:

- *Nessus.*
  https://www.tenable.com/products/nessus-
  vulnerability-scanner.
- *Nexpose.*
  https://www.rapid7.com/products/nexpose/.
- *OpenVAS.* http://www.openvas.org/.

Installing Nessus

There are two available versions of **Nessus**: a paid one and a free one. We will obviously refer to the second one.

We start by going to
https://www.tenable.com/products/nessus-
vulnerability-scanner and downloading this software.

At this stage we need to obtain an activation code that validates the license we are using. Just click on "Get an Activation Code" as you can see from the screenshot here below:

You will receive an e-mail with the activation code within a short period of time. Once the installation is complete, a browser window will open and point to: **http://127.0.0.1:8834.**

You will then need to enter the activation code that was provided to you:

If all went well, we should now be able to start using this software.

Scanning With Nessus

Nessus has a set of pre-compiled scans that you just need to execute:

We can use KFSensor to test the vulnerabilities of our victim machine.

Once scanned, this is the first detected vulnerability:

More in detail:

To confirm this, we can verify that the service is simulated on KFSensor:

Below is an overview of the vulnerabilities found:

An interesting feature is the possibility to create an exportable report in .pdf format:

Installing Nexpose

At this step, we need to download the Nexpose software and type the free license key.

We can run this software by connecting to the following link: **https: // localhost: 3780.**

Once we open this software, we can perform various actions:

Scanning With Nexpose

The first action we need to take is to create a site:

We can specify the type of scan to be performed:

The scan results can be summarized as follows:

In the image below we can see a detailed list of the vulnerabilities found:

Nexpose offers us the possibility to create easy interactions with, for example, Metasploit.

We can also see enough details about each vulnerability:

We are also provided with suggestions regarding the remediation phase, which is meant to find a remedy to the vulnerabilities found:

Here too, we have the possibility to generate a customizable report:

Websites For Vulnerability Search

Here is a list of websites you can refer to for more details about each vulnerability:

- *Exploit Database.* https://www.exploit-db.com/.
- *Security Focus.* http://www.securityfocus.com/.
- *Packet Storm.* https://packetstormsecurity.com/.
- *CVE Details.* http://www.cvedetails.com/.

Chapter 17 Learning How to Carry Out an Effective Attack

Now that you have a good understanding of hacking concepts and what is involved in the penetration of a system as well as how you can turn hacking into a career, we want to get into the heart of the action and learning how to carry out an effective attack. This is for demonstration purposes to help strengthen your knowledge and ideally stem further education. If you are still unsure on the basics of hacking, have a read through and study this book thoroughly as we will be going through this step by step guide with the assumption that you have a solid grasp of the topics of hacking and computer security and we wouldn't want you to get lost along the way.

Before you do get started, you will need to utilize a tool to help with the pen-test. For this example, we will be using Metasploit, an open source tool which has a number of functions which pen-testers and black hat hackers alike will find incredibly useful. The tool has a database filled with a large number of known exploits which can be picked up during the vulnerability test by the variety of scanners. Metasploit is one of the more popular pen-testing software applications and as an open source program, there is a large community which you can interact with in case you have any questions or concerns.

For the purpose of this example, we will be hacking into a virtual machine as this is a great way to practice and scan for weaknesses without actually breaking into an established machine. We will be scanning our virtual machine for exploits upon which we will then penetrate the system and extract the information we require. The virtual machine will also have limited access meaning it won't actually be accessible as easy to other people who may be scanning your network, leaving you in complete control. In order to create a virtual machine, we will be using VirtualBox, a software that allows you to establish a hacking lab in order to test your skills on a simulated machine. VirtualBox is another open source software that allows you to have access to the source code free of charge, allowing you to customise your build to your specifications.

Before continuing with your experiment ensure that the techniques and tools you use throughout this test are confined only to your machine and never used on other computers as this is not only illegal, it is also potentially dangerous. Even if you are simply learning how to carry out an attack for the purpose of your own education, if you are caught you can be prosecuted, and as you should have a good understanding from reading this book, this can be quite a serious crime and yes, it is possible to be caught. Keeping this in mind, let us go through with our virtual pen-test.

Initial Preparation

The first step toward setting up your environment is creating virtual machine to run on VirtualBox. You will need two machines, a target and a victim. You are able to download these online, they will come with files that we can extract as well as vulnerabilities to exploit. Once you have the files in place, extract them and create a new machine on VirtualBox and choose the type of machine you will be using. From there you decide how much RAM your machine will be running with, this isn't too important so selecting a small amount won't affect your test, 512MB is a good starting point.

Your next task is then to select a hard disk by checking the Use an Existing Disk option. You are able to click on the folder option and select the appropriate file that you had extracted from your download files and once that is all done, click create and your virtual machine and you are ready to move onto the next step.

Creating a Network

In order to access your machine, you will need to establish a virtual network. This is to keep your machine safe from existing threats outside your control. You are able to do this through VirtualBox by going through File > Preferences > Network > Host Only Network. Once you click the plus sign, you are able to add a new entry which will be your virtual network. Now is time to add your virtual machine to the virtual network. You are able to do this by selecting your virtual machine and clicking settings from the menu. From there you will see the network tab which will allow you to click 'Attacked to' from and Host-Only Adaptor from the drop-down menu.

Attacking Tools

Now that your network and machine have been set up it is time to acquire the tools to launch your attack. In this example, we will be using Kali as it is simple to set up and you can also run it live in a virtual machine. Once you have downloaded Kali as an ISO file, open VirtualBox and click Add to allow you to create another machine which will be your attacker. For your attacker, you want to allocate some more memory to the machine of around 2GB, if your machine has less than 4GB on the system, you may need to allocate less. You will not need to allocate any hard drive space, Kali is running live so check the box Do Not Add a Virtual Hard Drive. Once you are ready, hit create and your offending machine will be created. Ensure that you attach the machine to your network and change the adapter to host-holy. From here, you will start both machines and run Kali on your attack machine when prompted to add a bootable CD. You are then presented with the interface, and are ready to start scanning and gathering information from the Kali desktop interface.

Gathering Information

The next step in carrying out your attack is deciding upon your target. For the purpose of this experiment, we will be carrying out the attack on our victim server. In reality, this is a simple surface attack rather than focusing on the entire network that we had set up or the virtualization tools. From there it is time to gather information to discover the vulnerabilities that we will be exploiting. In order to do this, we will need to set this up in the software. This is where Metasploit will come into play as our framework for carrying out the pen-test, taking us through the process.

It is now time to begin collecting information. To do this, we must first we must initiate the services through Kali by entering:

"service postgresql start"

"service metasploit start"

Metasploit is best used through the console interface known as MSFConsole which is opened with

"Msfconsole"

Now you are ready to start your scan.

Scanning for Ports

In order to gather information on ports, you can use Nmap which is built into MSFconsole. In order to set this up, you will first need to enter the IP address of the target which you can find by typing in

"ifconfig"

This will then bring up information on the IP address, labelled inet addr within the eth0 block. The IP address should be similar to other machines found on your network. By running a scan of the IP address by using

Db_map -sS -A *TARGET IP ADDRESS*

You are able to have detailed list of all services running on the machine. From there you are able gather further information on each of the services to discover any vulnerabilities to exploit. Once you have found the weakest point, you are able to move into attack mode.

Exploitation

By enter services into MSFconsole, you are able to access the database of information on the services running on the machine. Once you have discovered a service that is particularly vulnerable, you are able to scan this service to assess points of weakness. This is done by typing

Search *service name*

Once you have done this, you will be provided a list of exploits which you can take advantage and can then tell MSFconsole to exploit the model. Once you have set the target, you simply need to type the command "run" for the program to work its magic and access the port. You will then be able to see what you are able to do once operating from the computer with a number of commands at your disposal with the permissions provided to you by the service. From here you are able to extract data as well as upload data depending on your objective.

Once you have accessed the machine, you will obviously want to ensure that you remained in control and fortunately Metasploit has a number of tools to assist.

Having a deeper understanding of the meaning behind the word hacker can open up new doors for you not just within your career if you decide to explore IT security but also within your business and personal life as you become better equipped in dealing with external threats to your networks and systems. Before reading this book, you like many other people, may have had some misconceptions about what hacking actually means, who is behind it, why they do it, what they have to gain from it and what can be done to prevent them.

Now that you have reached the end of our book on hacking, you should have a much greater insight into the world of hacking including what it means to be an ethical hacker and how they operate. Knowing that an ethical hacker is also known as a white hat hacker, you also learnt the difference between white and black hat hackers, who are motivated by personal reasons whether that could be financial or ideological. You also gained some insight into the hackers that lie on the boundaries of ethics such as those known as grey hats and red hats as well the hacktivists that so often capture our awareness in the media.

We also explored the techniques used by hackers to attack your computer and what each of these attacks can do to a system, the seriousness behind them and the types of hackers that employ these tactics to achieve their motivations. Upon learning these techniques, you also learnt how it was possible to avoid becoming a target through precautions which can protect your system and the information contained on it.

We then moved onto the topic on penetration testing and how organizations are able to simulate attacks on their own systems in order to expose weaknesses and vulnerabilities that could be exploited by external hackers. We learnt the basic process of how a pen-test works and why it is performed. This gave us some insight into the world of ethical hackers and what their job is comprised of. Once learning this, we took a deeper look into careers in IT security, how the indri is moving and the qualifications that are widely recognised in the industry.

We then took a look at the other side of the coin into the world of cyber terrorism. We explored the reasoning's behind why terrorists carry out these attacks as well as how organizations are able to better equip themselves for dealing with these threats. In looking at each type of attack, we gained an understand how businesses need to be extra vigilant to avoid suffering losses both financial and intangible.

Towards the end of the book we walked through the basic setup of a pen-test and how it can be performed using a lab type scenario on a virtual machine. While this was just a brief cover of a pen-test, it hopefully spurred some curiosity for you to continue your education further and develop new skills in hacking. With the now solid understanding of hacking in your possession, it is worth exploring further certifications and courses that will allow you to get closer to a career in security as a white hat hacker and expressing your skills in a healthy environment or just to expand your knowledge and become more aware.

Conclusion

I want to thank you once again for choosing this book.

Kali Linux is a very advanced flavor of Linux, which is used for Security Auditing and Penetration Testing. After all the tools that we have looked at, it is pretty clear that if you want to succeed in the domain of Security Research, Kali Linux will provide with unlimited power to achieve the same. It is also clear that if you are just beginning with Linux, Kali Linux is not the place that you would want to start with as it is a highly complex operating system created and aimed at achieving one goal and that is security.